Part B Units 7–12

Upper-I

Student's Book

New Headway
English Course

Liz & John Soars

University of Chi.
Bognor Regis Campus
Upper Bognor Road, Bognor Regis
West Sussex PO21 1HR

This book is dedicated to the memory
of John Haycraft, founder of the
International House organization, who
inspired so much in so many in the field
of English Language teaching.

Oxford University Press 1998

Contents

LANGUAGE INPUT

SKILLS DEVELOPMENT

● Reading	● Speaking	● Listening	● Writing
Letters between Sean and his grandmother – an exercise on verb patterns pp 68, 70 'The family who turned back the clock' – a family who give up all domestic appliances for three days p 72	Discussion – domestic life fifty years ago – things you couldn't live without p 72 Discussion – the pros and cons of television p 75	A song – *Fast car*, by Tracy Chapman p 75 T7.5	Contrasting ideas *whereas* *However* *although* Writing about an invention you couldn't live without p 75
'Jane Austen, the hottest writer in Hollywood' – the famous English novelist who is enjoying a revival p 82	Talking about the lives of famous people p 81 Discussion – the lives of women past and present p 83	One side of a phone conversation p 80 T8.1 An interview with Tim Rice, who wrote the lyrics to *Jesus Christ Superstar*, and Paul Nicholas, who played Jesus p 85 T8.7	Writing a fan letter p 86
'Mysteries of the universe' – puzzles that have plagued human beings for thousands of years p 91	General knowledge quiz p 89 Discussion – retelling a story from another point of view p 95	'Saying *I won't*' – a radio programme about people who change their mind at the altar p 95 T9.6 A song – *Waiting at the church* p 95 T9.7	Joining sentences Conjunctions *whenever unless* Adverbs *anyway actually* p 96
'Living history' – the 100-year-old lady who lives in the past p 98 'People and their money' – who's rich and who's poor these days? (jigsaw) p 103	Giving a short talk about your first friend or teacher p 100 Attitudes to money p 102 Homelessness p 105	Homelessness – interviews with people who live on the streets, and those who try to help them p 105 T10.4	Writing about a period in history p 106
'Who's life's perfect anyway?' – two people's lives p 109 'Things we never said' – a short story about a failed relationship, by Fiona Goble p 112	Roleplay – two lovers tell each other the truth p 113 Acting out a dramatic scene p 116	A radio play, based on the text 'Things we never said' p 111 T11.4 'Family secrets' – two people talk about a secret in their lives p 115 T11.5	Writing a play with stage directions p 116
'Michelangelo' – one of the world's greatest artists p 118 'It blows your mind!' – eye-witness accounts of the first atomic explosion p 121	Discussion – famous photos of the twentieth century p 124 Discussion – how the atomic bomb changed history p 123	Children's jokes p 124 T12.4 Various people describe great events of the twentieth century p 125 T12.5	Describing a career Word order and focus of attention p 126

Phonetic symbols (inside back cover)

Doing without

Verb patterns
Soundbites

1 Complete the following sentences about yourself.

a I'm good at …
b I find it difficult …
c I enjoy …
d I'm interested in …
e I can't stand …
f I like …
g I'd like …
h I can't afford …
i I'm thinking of …
j I'm looking forward to …
k I always forget …
l Our teacher always makes us …

2 Read your sentences aloud to the rest of the class.

3 Which sentences did you complete with the *-ing* form of a verb? Which did you complete with the infinitive?

LANGUAGE IN CONTEXT

Verb patterns

1 **T 7.1** Sean /ʃɔːn/, aged eight, lives in Brighton on the south coast of England. He has written to his grandmother, who lives far away in the north. Read and listen to his letter.

Hello.

Friday after school

Dear Grandma,
    How are you? I am well. Liam is well, too. Mummy says perhaps you can help me do something for my school. You see, my teacher told us to find out about the olden days - you know a long long time ago when you were eight like me. Miss Bixby (she's our teacher) says it's a good idea to ask somebody really old to tell us about it. Please, please, please Grandma, will you write and tell me? Daddy says there was a war and you can remember being there. Is this true? Is it difficult for you to remember? I'd love to hear about it. I love hearing stories about when you were little like me.
    Liam is crying. He's fallen over again. He's nearly learnt to walk but not yet. He's noisy and makes a mess. Mummy makes me play with him but I hate playing with him. He's no good at playing.
    Grandma, please write to me. I want to see you very, very soon.

Waaah.

Lots and lots and lots of love and kisses.
Sean xxxxxxx

P.S. Don't forget to send me a birthday present.

2 Read the sentences about Sean's letter. Tick the verbs or phrases below which can fill the gap correctly. Cross-out the verb or verbs which cannot.

Example
Sean is writing to his grandmother because he _____ help him with some schoolwork.
1 wants to   2 wants her to ✓
3 needs her to ✓

a His mother thinks that his grandmother will _____ do it.
1 help him   2 agree to   3 enjoy

b Miss Bixby _____ the children to do the homework.
1 has told   2 said   3 expects

c She has _____ them to talk to an old person.
1 suggested   2 advised   3 encouraged

d Sean begs his grandmother _____ about the war.
1 to tell   2 to tell him   3 telling him

e Sean wonders if his grandmother has difficulty _____ the war.
1 to remember   2 in remembering   3 remembering

f He'd like _____ stories about the war.
1 to hear   2 hearing   3 her to tell him

g He always enjoys _____ his grandmother talking about her childhood.
1 to listen to   2 listening to   3 hearing

h Sean _____ play with his little brother.
1 is made   2 is told to   3 is made to

i He _____ playing with Liam.
1 can't stand   2 doesn't want   3 dislikes

j Liam _____ to walk.
1 is trying   2 isn't able   3 can't

k Sean's looking forward _____ his grandmother soon.
1 to seeing   2 to see   3 seeing

l He _____ her to send him a birthday present.
1 remembers   2 reminds   3 asks

3 Match a pattern in **A** with a sentence in **B**.

A	B
verb + -ing	She **wants to go** to the cinema.
verb + infinitive (with *to*)	It's **impossible to stop** her.
verb + sb + infinitive (with *to*)	I'm interested **in coming**.
verb + sb + infinitive (without *to*)	She **wants you to take** her.
adjective + infinitive	She's **finished doing** her homework.
preposition + -ing	I won't **let her go** out.

● Grammar questions

– Which of the verb patterns in Exercise 3 can you identify in Exercise 2?
– Which can you identify in Sean's letter?
  Read it again and underline them.

PRACTICE BANK

1 Grandma's reply

1 Read Grandma's letter to Sean. Put the verb in brackets into the correct form.

22 St Bede's Terrace,
Newcastle-upon-Tyne.
Tuesday

My dear Sean,
How lovely (a)_____ (get) your letter! Mummy is right! I will really enjoy (b)_____ (help) you with your schoolwork, and I will try very hard (c)_____ (remember) what it was like when I was a little girl all those years ago.
When the war started, I was just five and I'll never forget (d)_____ (watch) grandfather dig a big black hole in the back garden. This was our air raid shelter. At first I was really scared of (e)_____ (go) into it. Every time the siren went off, I started (f)_____ (tremble) and I was sick, actually sick with fear. I refused (g)_____ (leave) my bed. I didn't find it easy (h)_____ (sleep) in that shelter. But soon, (i)_____ (get) used to (j)_____ (live) in the cities was so dangerous that the government decided (k)_____ (send) all the children away to the countryside. I think I was lucky because I was able (l)_____ (go away) to my aunt's. Some children were forced (m)_____ (stay) with total strangers. My aunt lived in a small town, called Alston, high in the hills, not too far from Newcastle. And guess what, Sean, she had a sweet shop! Mrs Crozier's Sweet Shop. But, oh dear me, at first I was so unhappy, I couldn't stop (n)_____ (cry) because I couldn't help (o)_____ (worry) about my mother back home. My aunt let me (p)_____ (have) as many sweets as I wanted, but I was too miserable (q)_____ (eat) many. Silly me! Most children didn't have the chance of (r)_____ (get) lots of sweets because sweets were rationed. That meant that you couldn't buy all you wanted. You were only allowed (s)_____ (buy) a small amount. Lots of other things were rationed, too. It was almost impossible (t)_____ (get) butter, cream, meat, fruit, vegetables, and petrol. We did without a lot of things during the war. Can you believe that just after it ended, someone gave me a banana and I didn't know what (u)_____ (do) with it?
Sean, I hope this is useful. I'm longing (v)_____ (see) you all. Give my love to Mummy, Daddy and Liam. Don't worry, he'll be much more fun soon.
Lots of love and kisses,

Grandma xxx

2 **T 7.2** Listen and check your answers.

2 Discussing grammar

Match a line on the left with a line on the right.

a They stopped playing football | because they were tired of working.
   They stopped to play football | because it got dark.

b I simply don't remember giving | you any money yesterday.
   Please remember to give | my best wishes to your parents.

c Try counting | from 1 to 10 in Arabic. I bet you can't!
   Try to count | sheep if you can't get to sleep.

d We prefer staying at the Ritz | whenever we're in London.
   We'd prefer to stay at the Ritz | next time we're in London.

e He seems to drink too much. | He's fallen asleep.
   He seems to be drinking too much. | He's rarely sober.
   He seems to have drunk too much. | He's swaying.

f I like going | home now, please.
   I like to go | to the cinema.
   I'd like to go | to the dentist twice a year.

١, ٢, ٣, ٤, ٥,
٦, ٧, ٨, ٩, ١٠

3 *We'd love to!*

1 Sometimes the whole infinitive need not be repeated if it is understood.

   Example
   A Can you and Mary come to lunch next Sunday?
   B Oh yes, we'd *love to* .

   Write a reply to **A**, using the verb in brackets.

a A Are we going to have a break?

   B No, _____ (not have time).

b A Can I smoke in here?

   B No, _____ (not allow).

c A I can't help you do your homework this evening. Sorry.

   B Oh, but _____ (promise).

d A Why did you do Exercise 2?

   B Because you _____ (tell).

e A You said you'd phone me last night.

   B I'm really sorry, _____ (mean), but I forgot.

f A Have you finished marking the homework yet?

   B Sorry, _____ (not have a chance).

2 T 7.3 Listen and check your answers. Practise the conversations with a partner. Pay particular attention to the stress and intonation.

LANGUAGE REVIEW

Verb patterns

-*ing* form

The -*ing* form of the verb can be used …

1 … after certain verbs.
   I *love hearing* stories about when you were little.
   He *can't stand playing* with his brother.

2 … after prepositions.
   I'm good *at cooking*.
   After leaving school, I went to university.

3 … as the subject of a sentence.
   Living in the cities was so dangerous.
   Smoking is bad for your health.

Infinitives

Infinitives are used …

1 … after certain verbs.
   What are you *planning to do*?
   We *can't afford to go* out very often.

2 … after certain adjectives.
   I find it *difficult to make* new friends.

-*ing* or infinitive?

With some verbs there is no change in meaning.

It *started raining/to rain*.

With some verbs there is a change in meaning.

I tried *to put* out the fire. (This was my objective.)
I tried *pouring* water on it. (This was my method.)

📖 Grammar Reference: page 137.

READING AND SPEAKING

Pre-reading task

Use your dictionary to help with new words.

1 Which of the following household items do you think were in use fifty years ago?
Which do you have in your home?

personal computer	fridge
camcorder	electric razor
radio	washing machine
video recorder	deep freeze
tin opener	microwave oven
CD player	food processor
tumble drier	music system
iron	cassette recorder
vacuum cleaner	dishwasher
word processor	jacuzzi
television	mobile phone

2 Imagine life in your family fifty years ago. How did your parents and grandparents live? How was their daily life different from today?

3 If you lived then, what would you miss about your life today? What wouldn't you miss? Write two lists. Compare your ideas with your partner and the rest of the class.

Reading

You are going to read about the Jones family. Read the text quickly, then discuss these questions.

1 Identify the people in the main picture. How do you know who's who?

2 What was the experiment that they agreed to do?

3 Which of the items in the box above are mentioned in the article? Underline those which are.

The family who turned back the clock

THE JONES FAMILY HAVE NINE TV SETS, SIX COMPUTERS, THREE CARS, AND EVERY DOMESTIC APPLIANCE. What would their life be like without them? Melanie Adams reports

When Malcolm Jones woke up last Monday, he heard the birds singing. Not remarkable, you might think, especially given that he lives near a
5 forest. But birdsong in the Jones household is usually drowned by a tidal wave of electronic music crashing around the house as soon as his four children wake up.
10 This is a family who have chosen to fill their home with every conceivable gadget. They have nine television sets, including one in each bedroom and in the kitchen. All the children have
15 their own personal computers and CD players. Of course, there are all the usual appliances we all take for granted, such as the washing machine, tumble drier, dishwasher, deep freeze, microwave oven,
20 and video recorder, but they also have an electric trouser press, two power showers, an Olympic-sized spa bath and jacuzzi, three cars, and a music system which plays throughout the whole house.

The experiment

25

What happens if all the props of modern living are removed?

To help us find out, we asked the Joneses to turn back the clock fifty
30 years and to switch off all their labour-saving gadgets and push-button entertainment for three days. We also wanted them to stop using their cars. The family, comprising Malcolm, 48,
35 Carol, 43, and their four children Emma, 17, Richard, 14, Tamsin, 9, and Tom, 7, were not enthusiastic, but everyone, except for Emma, agreed to try. (She

couldn't stand the thought of being
40 without the telephone and her car, which she had only just learnt to drive, so she refused point-blank to join in.) The other three children were not allowed to use their computers or watch TV. They
45 were banned from opening the freezer to get out fish fingers and oven chips. Malcolm was forbidden to use his electric razor and mobile phone, but allowed to use his car for work. Carol
50 was encouraged to go everywhere on foot or by bicycle (women rarely drove 50 years ago), told to ignore the washing machine and dishwasher, and she was discouraged from using the telephone.

How did they cope?

The much-dreaded three days got under way!

Old-fashioned meals, games, and entertainment were planned for the evenings. After eating together at the kitchen table, they sat playing cards, putting off doing the washing-up because they all hated doing that.

Carol was surprised at how long everything took. 'By the time I had washed up the breakfast things and got back from walking the children to school, it was nearly lunchtime. Getting to the shops, which normally takes five minutes in the car, took at least an hour, so it was impossible just to pop out for a loaf of bread. It was strange having to wait until the washing dried in the garden before getting the ironing done, instead of simply using the drier.'

Although Carol found it quite difficult to get used to the length of time it took to do things, she enjoyed having a slower, more relaxed pace of life. Also, the lack of electronic entertainment, particularly the TV, had a dramatic effect on the children. They got on much better together and seemed to enjoy each other's company more, although they clearly believed that they were suffering. Tamsin even spent some time gazing at the blank TV screen in her bedroom.

'All sorts of things that we had put off doing got done,' said Carol. 'Bikes got mended, rooms tidied, bookshelves sorted, hamsters cleaned out. Tamsin and Tom started to play games together and even read stories to each other.'

What did they think?

What Malcolm liked most was the peace. 'I usually start the day by watching the business news on TV from bed. Then I press the music button while I shower and get dressed. I didn't miss any of this, I just enjoyed hearing the birds singing and chatting to Carol. I think the whole experience did the children a lot of good. If it were my decision now, I'd throw all the televisions away.'

The children vigorously denied that any good had been done to them. Richard spoke for them all when he said, 'It was awful. I missed my music, I missed the computer games, and I missed the TV. We had to read *books* instead!'

Carol's feelings were the most ambiguous. 'I enjoyed doing more things together as a family. But as the housewife, I didn't like my day being so full of household chores. When you've got a dishwasher, you stack it as you go through the day and turn it on at night. But you can't leave dirty dishes in the sink all day, so you've got to keep doing the washing-up. Also, without a phone and a car, I felt really isolated.'

All of this just goes to show that, fascinating as the experiment was, you cannot turn the clock back. This is doubtless a big relief to the Jones children!

Comprehension check

Work in groups. Read the article again and answer the questions.

1 What is the first thing the children usually do when they wake up in the morning?

2 What does this family own which is more than the average family owns?

3 What were some of the rules of the experiment for each member of the family?

4 Who refused to join in the experiment? Why?
Who enjoyed the experiment most? Why? Who enjoyed it least? Why? Who had mixed feelings? Why?

5 Choose one member of the Jones family and imagine you are him/her. Describe your typical day to the others in your group.

'Well, the first thing I usually do when I wake up is …'

Now describe a day for the same person during the experiment.

'During the experiment, when I woke up I wasn't allowed to … , so …'

6 **T 7.4** Which member of the family is most likely to have said the following? Why?

a There's no way I'm going to give up using my car!

b It's a beautiful morning, isn't it dear?

c No, I haven't ironed your white shirt yet! I haven't had the time.

d Come on! Stop gazing at that blank screen. Let's have a game of Scrabble.

e Well, I'm not doing it! I did it last night. Anyway, I want to mend the puncture on my bike.

f Damn! I forgot to buy sugar!

g If it were up to me, I'd throw the lot out!

h Personally, I think life was much harder fifty years ago.

i Never again! That was the longest three days of my life!

Practise saying their comments with appropriate stress and intonation.

Language work

1 Put the following phrases from the text into your own words.

a … birdsong … is usually drowned by a tidal wave of electronic music crashing around the house … (l. 5–8)

b … fill their home with every conceivable gadget. (l. 11–12)

c … the usual appliances we all take for granted … (l. 16–17)

d … the props of modern living … (l. 26–7)

e … labour-saving gadgets and push-button entertainment … (l. 31–2)

f … she refused point-blank … (l. 42)

g The much-dreaded three days … (l. 56)

h … the lack of … the TV, had a dramatic effect on the children. (l. 79–81)

i The children vigorously denied that any good had been done to them. (l. 105–6)

j This is doubtless a big relief to the Jones children! (l. 124–6)

2 Go through the text and <u>underline</u> all the verb patterns with -ing forms and infinitives.

● VOCABULARY AND LISTENING

Hot Verbs (3): get

1 The verb *get* is very common in spoken English. It has many different uses. Here are some examples from the text about the Jones family.

a You**'ve got** a dishwasher.

b I **got back** from walking the children to school.

c She found it difficult to **get used to** the length of time things took.

d You**'ve got to** keep doing the washing-up.

e All sorts of things **got done**.

f They **got on** much better **together**.

Replace the words in bold with one of the expressions below in the correct tense.

> have to   become accustomed to
> be done (passive)   return   have/own
> have a (better) relationship

2 Write answers to the following questions about yourself.

a Have you got a pet/a CD player?

b What have you got to do when you get home tonight?

c How do you get to school?

d What time do you usually get to school?

e How many TV channels can you get?

f When did you last get angry? Why?

g How do you get on with your parents?

h How often do you get your hair cut?

i In what ways is your English getting better?

Compare your answers with a partner. Work together to rewrite the questions without using *get*.

Phrasal verbs with *get*

Get can combine with particles to make phrasal verbs.

1 Complete each group of sentences with one of the particles from the box below. (Careful, only six of the particles are used.)

> at   away   into   off   on   out   over   round   through   up

a You always get | of doing the washing-up. It's not fair.
  How did our secret get | ? Everyone knows now!
  I got a great book | of the library. You can borrow it.

b You're always getting | me! Leave me alone!
  The detective got | the truth through careful questioning.
  I can't get | the sugar. It's right at the back.

c It took me ages to get | the operation.
  He couldn't get his point | to me at first so he explained it again.
  I can't get | how much your children have grown.

d Sam is always getting | to something naughty!
  We got | to page 56 in the last lesson.
  I had to get | at 5 a.m. to catch the plane.

e I couldn't get | to Joe. I don't think his phone's working.
  We got | a huge amount of money in Paris.
  I failed, but Sue got | the exam with flying colours.

f She couldn't get her ring | her finger because it was so swollen.
  Oliver finally got | with Claire at Stuart's party.
  Ben stole a car but he got | lightly because he was only sixteen.

2 There are four more particles in the box. All of them combine with *get*. Choose one of them, and research the meanings in your dictionary. Tell the rest of the class what you find out.

Listening

Fast Car–a song by Tracy Chapman

1 **T 7.5** Here are some lines from a song called *Fast Car* by Tracy Chapman. Listen and complete the gaps. They all contain expressions with *get*.

You _____ a fast car.
Maybe together we can
_____
But me myself _____.
I've got a plan to _____
You and I can both _____
You see my old man _____
I said somebody _____
We _____ a decision
I know things will _____
You'll find work and I'll
_____

And I _____ that pays all
our bills
I _____ and I ain't going
nowhere

2 Listen again and read the tapescript on page 128 to check your answers.

WRITING AND DISCUSSION

Contrasting ideas

1 How often do you watch television? Which are your most and least favourite programmes?
One half of the class make a list of all the *good* points about TV. The other half make a list of only the *bad* points. Compare your ideas.

2 Join the ideas in **A** and **C** with the correct linking words in **B**. Change the punctuation where necessary.

A	B	C
I always watch the news on TV	even though whereas	John always watches sport. it's usually depressing.
He writes all personal letters by hand	although despite	he has a computer. having a computer.
It took only an hour to get to the airport	However, in spite of	the traffic. they still missed the plane.
Some couples argue all the time	Nevertheless, whereas	others never do. their marriages still work.
Kathy rarely uses her mobile phone	However, even though	Kevin uses his all the time. she has one.

Look again at the lists of good and bad points about TV. Join some of them with some of the words in **B**.

3 Complete the following statements in a suitable way.

a His idea is brilliant in theory. However, it …
b My brothers love playing computer games, whereas I …
c On the one hand, cars are really convenient to get you from A to B, but on …
d I'm going to drive into London, even though …
e Foreign travel is very exciting, but at the same time it …
f The critics slammed Ed Newhart's latest film. Nevertheless, …
g Their daughter is often sullen and moody, despite always …

4 Which modern inventions would you find it most difficult to live without? Discuss your ideas with a partner.

Choose *one* invention which you feel is very necessary to your life (it could be anything from the Internet to an electric toothbrush) and answer the following questions about it.

– What invention have you chosen and why?
– What are its advantages? Compare these with any disadvantages.
– Why is it important to you? Give your personal opinion.
– Write some final concluding comments.

First make notes, then expand the notes into an essay of about 200–300 words.

PostScript

Soundbites

1 Where would you hear the following? Who is speaking to who?

> OK, folks. Don't go away now. We'll be back in a few minutes just after the break.

> With respect to my Right Honourable friend, I have to say that I find his statement to be inconsistent with the truth.

> *It's not fair! Everyone else is allowed to go.*

> *Ooh! Hear, hear!*

> *I don't care about everyone else. You're not, and that's all there is to it.*

> *Things aren't what they used to be.*

> *You can say that again. It was different in our day, wasn't it?*

> Open wide and say 'Ah'. Oh, dear.

> Ish it bad newsh?

> Will passengers in rows A to K please board now?

> A big Mac with regular fries and a strawberry milkshake.

> *I can't find my gym kit.*

> Eat here or take away?

> *Think. Where did you last have it?*

> **Mummy! I need a wee-wee!**

> News is coming in of a major hold-up on the A45 Colchester bypass. Drivers are advised to avoid this area if at all possible.

> Has Kelly Jones' latest album been released yet?

> *Could you develop this for me?*

> Well, I'm just going to put my feet up and have a nap, if that's all right with you.

> Normal six by four?

> *Yeah, that's fine.*

> When do you want them by?

> Let passengers off first. Move right down inside the car.

> *This time tomorrow's all right.*

2 **T 7.6** Listen to the dialogues.
Do the background noises help you to identify the situations?

> *Thanks for having me!*

> *'scuse fingers!*

8 Famous for fifteen minutes

Modal auxiliary verbs
Exaggeration and understatement

---

1 All modal verbs can be used to express degrees of probability.
Which of these sentences express probability? Put a ✔. Which don't? Put a ✗.

Example
She *must* be very rich. ✔ (probability)
You *must* do your homework. ✗

a We *might* go to Hawaii for our honeymoon.
b You *mustn't* smoke in this part of the restaurant.
c He *can't* be coming. It's already after ten o'clock.
d She *could* speak three languages fluently by the time she was five.

e He *could* be working in the library.
f The weather forecast says it *may* snow tomorrow.
g Good morning. *May* I speak to Mr Jones?
h *Will* you help me do my homework?
i That *will* be Ken on the phone. He promised to ring.
j You *should* see a doctor as soon as possible.
k It's eight o'clock. They *should* be arriving soon.
l They *must* have won the lottery.
m You *should* have told her the truth.

2 What concepts do the other sentences express?

Example
You *must* do your homework. (obligation)

LANGUAGE IN CONTEXT

Modal verbs of probability

1 Read the newspaper headlines. What do you think has happened to the man and the woman? Read the ideas below. Which do you agree with?

A
'Excuse me ... I've just jumped off the Empire State Building!'

He must be *Superman*!
He can't be serious. He must be joking.
He might be a bungee-jumper.
He could have come down by parachute.
He might have been trying to commit suicide.
He may be acting in a film.
He must have injured himself.
His story will be in all the newspapers.
He may become famous.

B
40 YEARS IN BED – WITH FLU

She probably doesn't have flu. (can't)
_____

It's likely that she has had a more serious illness. (must)
_____

Perhaps she is just very lazy. (might)
_____

It's not possible that the doctor told her to stay in bed for so long. (couldn't)
_____

Surely someone has been looking after her. (must)
_____

She will probably find it very difficult to walk again. (may)
_____

2 Rewrite the ideas in **B** using the modal verb in brackets.

3 Read the complete newspaper stories. Which of the ideas in **A** and **B** were correct? Answer these questions.

a Why did Jason jump off the Empire State Building? Why has Mrs Teppit spent forty years in bed?

b Who are the other people in the stories? What did they do?

Other uses of modal verbs

1 All of the comments below were made by people in the two newspaper stories. Who do you think is speaking to who?

'Excuse me. *May* I come in?'

'You *must* stay in bed until I return.'

'I*'ve had to* look after her since I was 14.'

'I *couldn't* believe my eyes.'

'You *should have been* examined years ago.'

'She *won't* get up.'

'I *can't* find anything wrong with you at all.'

'I *ought to* call the police.'

'*Can* I get up soon?'

'You *should* try to lose weight.'

'She told me that I *couldn't* get married and that I *had to* look after her.'

'*Will* you spend Christmas with us?'

'You*'ll have to* have physiotherapy.'

'You *mustn't* do anything like this again.'

'You *don't have to* do everything for her.'

2 What concepts do the verbs in italics express? Permission? Obligation/advice? Ability? Willingness/refusal?

'Excuse me ... I've just jumped off the Empire State Building!'

On Christmas Eve, Bob Stichman was working in his office on the 85th floor of the Empire State Building in New York, when he heard a knock at the window. He looked up and saw a man standing on the window ledge asking to come in. 'I thought I was dreaming. You don't meet a lot of guys coming in through the window of the 85th floor!' The guy was Jason Hosen, a young, unsuccessful artist, who was so broke and alone that he had decided to kill himself. He had taken the elevator to the 86th floor and then hurled himself towards the tiny cars 1,000 feet below on Fifth Avenue. However, strong winds had blown him onto the window ledge of the 85th floor, which is where he met Bob Stichman. His story appeared on TV, and hundreds of people have offered to have him stay for Christmas.

40 YEARS IN BED – WITH FLU

Doctor Mark Pemberton, who has just taken over a medical practice in rural Suffolk, visited a 74-year-old widow, Mrs Ada Teppit at her home in the village of Nacton. Mrs Teppit has been bedridden for 40 years. The doctor examined her but couldn't find anything wrong. He questioned her daughter, Norma, aged 54, and to his amazement discovered that 40 years ago the village doctor had ordered Mrs Teppit to bed because she had influenza and told her not to get up until he returned. He never returned so she never got up. She has never married nor had any job other than taking care of her mother. Her daughter has been looking after her ever since. She has never married nor had any job other than taking care of her mother. Her muscles have wasted, and she has put on a lot of weight. She may never walk again. Now Mrs Teppit's

● Grammar questions

– Which of these statements express the greatest degree of certainty? Which express less certainty? Which expresses the least?

*That **'ll**/**won't** be the postman.*
*That **must**/**can't** be the postman.*
*That **should** be the postman.*
*That **could**/**couldn't** be the postman.*
*That **may** be the postman.*
*That **might** be the postman.*

– All the above statements could be in answer to the question
*Who **is** that at the door?*
Change each one to answer the question
*Who **was** that at the door?*

– What is the past of these sentences?
He can see someone at the window.
She must call the doctor.
He has to tell the police.
She won't get out of bed.
You should call the police.
We needn't hurry. (Careful!)

PRACTICE BANK

1 Discussing grammar

1 Which of the words in the right hand column can fit into the sentences on the left? Sometimes several will fit. Discuss the possibilities with a partner.

a _____ I ask you a question about this exercise? **must**

b _____ you help me with this exercise, please? **can**

c He'll _____ hurry if he wants to get here in time. **may**

d I _____ be able to come round and see you tonight. **might**

e Sally _____ read when she was only three. **might**

f I _____ be seeing Theo later this evening, but I'm not sure. **could**

g You _____ be feeling very excited about your trip to Florida. **should**

h They _____ have finished dinner by now.

i You _____ pass the exam easily. You've worked really hard. **will/'ll**

j She always _____ leave work early on Fridays.

k That _____ be the taxi. **have/has to**

2 <u>Underline</u> the correct answer.

a I'm sorry I'm late, I *had to go/should have gone* to the post office.

b You *mustn't/don't have to* go to France to learn French, but it helps.

c You *mustn't/don't have to* drive if you've been drinking.

d I'm sorry. I *may not/cannot* be able to come to your party on Saturday.

e You lucky thing! How *could you/were you able to* get Madonna's autograph?

f I just waited outside the stage door and asked her if I *could/was able to* have it.

g The car *wouldn't/couldn't* start this morning, so I was late for work.

h I *wouldn't/couldn't* start the car this morning, so I was late for work.

i Do this exercise for homework. You *shouldn't/mustn't* have any problems with it.

j We *needn't have paid/didn't need to pay* to get into the museum. It was free.

2 Listening and speaking

1 **T 8.1** Listen to and read one side of
a telephone conversation, then answer
the questions below.

- Hello. Kingsbridge 810344. Rod speaking.
- Oh, hi Miranda. Why all the excitement?
- Yes, I can. I remember you doing it in
  the coffee bar. It was the one in the
  Daily Express, wasn't it? Didn't you have
  to name loads of capital cities?
- You can't have! I don't believe it.
  What's the prize?
- You must be kidding! That's brilliant.
  For how long?
- Well, you should be able to do quite a
  lot in three days. And the Waldorf
  Astoria! I'm impressed! Isn't that
  on Park Avenue?
- I thought so. Not that I've been there
  of course.
- And *what* could possibly be even
  better than that?
- Wow! That's fantastic. That's something
  I've always wanted to do. D'you know
  it only takes three and a half hours, so
  you arrive before you've left … if you see
  what I mean.
- You can't be serious? You know I'd
  love to! But why me? Surely you should
  be taking Richard.
- Oh, sorry! I didn't know. I really am sorry.
  When did this happen?…

Work in pairs. What deductions can you make about:
- the relationship between Miranda and Rod?
- the reason she is so excited?
- what she was doing in the coffee bar?
- where she is going?
- how she is travelling?
- the thing that Rod has always wanted to do?
- the relationship between Miranda and Richard?
- the future relationship between Miranda and Rod?

What do you think Miranda's exact words were in
the conversation?

2 **T 8.2** Listen to the full conversation between
Miranda and Rod. Were your deductions correct?

3 Go through the complete tapescript on page 138
and underline all the modal verbs.

3 Stress and intonation

Work in pairs. Take it in turns to be
A or B.

1 Student B should respond to A's
remarks using the words in brackets.
Make changes where necessary and
continue the conversations further.

Example
A I've never seen Tina eat meat.
B *I know. She must be a vegetarian.*
  (must, vegetarian)
A *But I've seen her eat fish.*

a A Oh no! I've lost my passport.
  B (could, leave, in the taxi)

b A It's an early start for us
    tomorrow.
  B (What time, have?)

c A The traffic's not moving. We'll
    never get to the concert.
  B (Don't worry, should, time)

d A I've brought you some flowers.
    I hope you like tulips.
  B (How kind, needn't)

e A All the teachers are going
    on strike!
  B (Brilliant, don't have, come,
    tomorrow)

2 **T 8.3** Listen to the sample answers,
paying particular attention to the stress
and intonation. Are they the same as
your replies?

LANGUAGE REVIEW

Modal auxiliary verbs

The main modal verbs are *must, can, could, may, might, should, ought to, will,* and *would*. All of these can be used to express degrees of certainty or probability. They also have other uses.

1 Degrees of certainty about the present

Certainty	She **will**	
	She **must**	
Possibility	She **could**	**be** at home.
	She **may**	**have** a high salary in that job.
	She **might**	**be earning** a lot of money. (continuous infinitive)
Certainty	She **should**	
	She **can't**	
	She **won't**	

2 Degrees of certainty about the past

Certainty	She **will**	
	She **must**	
Possibility	She **could**	**have been** at home. (perfect infinitive)
	She **may**	**have had** a high salary in that job.
	She **might**	**have been earning** a lot of money.
Certainty	She **should**	
	She **can't**	
	She **won't**	

3 Other uses of modal auxiliary verbs

Modal verbs also express concepts such as obligation (mild or strong), permission, ability, and willingness.

There are other verbs which express similar meanings. These are *have to, need to,* and *be able to*.

📖 **Grammar Reference: page 138.**

● READING AND SPEAKING

Get me Jane Austen's fax number!

Pre-reading task

1 What do you know about these people? Why are they famous? Were they famous in their lifetimes? Which of them do you think were rich as well as famous? Were their lives happy?

Jane Austen   **Marilyn Monroe**   Anne Frank

Mozart   *Shakespeare*   ANDY WARHOL

Eva Perón   Van Gogh

2 Look at the pictures of the two women. What do you think is the connection between them?

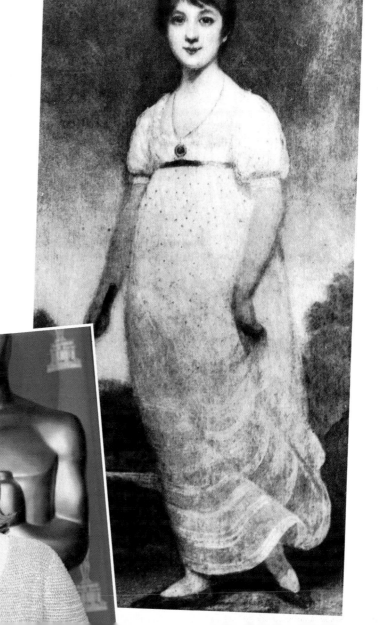

Reading

You are going to read about the English writer, Jane Austen (1775–1817). Since the age of cinema and television her novels have become more and more popular. Why do you think this is?

1 The following sentences have been removed from the text. Read them.
What do you learn about the life and work of Jane Austen?

a The family often had to entertain themselves at home.

b Jane Austen herself couldn't possibly have imagined this kind of worldwide fame.

c Jane must have felt particularly miserable at this time because she found it difficult to continue with her writing.

d Just as in most romantic novels, you may say, …

e By this time she was 27, and by the standards of the day, 'on the shelf'.

f They shouldn't have been written with the sole aim of commercial success.

g … which may have been started as early as 1793, …

2 Read the text. Where do the sentences go?

Jane Austen
– The hottest writer in
HOLLYWOOD

When the BBC screened its latest adaptation of Jane Austen's novel *Pride and Prejudice*, it was watched by a record 18 million British viewers. The series was then 5 sold to 18 countries round the world, from America to Australia, from Iceland to Israel. There are Jane Austen fans in all corners of the globe, and even special Jane Austen 10 discussion groups on the Internet.

(1) … In her lifetime she never once travelled abroad, indeed she hardly ever left the south of England. When she died a spinster, in 1817, only four of her 15 six novels had been published, all anonymously, and she had earned a grand total of £648.65 from her books. Now, nearly 200 years later, sales of her novels rival modern bestsellers such as 20 John le Carré, reaching 35,000 a week. There have been film and television productions of not only *Pride and Prejudice*, but also *Emma, Persuasion*, and the Oscar-winning *Sense and* 25 *Sensibility*. Her house in Chawton in Hampshire is visited by 200 people a day.

✄The secret of her success ✄

What makes her worldwide success so surprising is the narrowness of 30 **the world her stories portray,** 'three or four families in a country village,' as Jane Austen herself said. However, according to Nigel Nicolson, author of *The World of Jane Austen*, 35

the explanation for her enduring success is very simple: 'Her novels are love stories, always ending in a wedding. **They show a wonderful understanding of the little moves** 40 **that young people made then, and still do make, towards and away from each other.** They are also very funny.' Or, as the author P D James wrote, 'All the books have the same 45 basic plot – searching for and finding the right mate.' (2) … but the difference is that these were written by a genius.

✄The life and loves of Jane Austen ✄

She was born in 1775, the seventh of eight children. Her father was the Reverend George Austen. They were 55 not well off, and lived in a rambling rectory in the village of Steventon in the Hampshire hills. (3) … By the time she was 12, Jane was writing stories about heroines imprisoned in 60 haunted castles, being rescued by glamorous heroes.

In Jane's own life there were three romantic attachments. The first was a handsome Irish law student called 65 Tom Lefroy, who she met in 1795, but who had to return to Ireland a year

later. The second, in 1801, was a young man called Samuel Blackall, who she fell in love with when on holiday in Devon, but who tragically died suddenly, soon after. The third was a large young man called Harris Bigg-Wither, whose proposal she briefly accepted in 1802, but '**he had nothing to recommend him but his size**', so **she changed her mind**.

(4) ... She knew only too well that marriage was important for someone in her position, for the only work suitable for a penniless clergyman's daughter was school teaching or being a governess. Jane wrote to her niece: 'Single women have a dreadful propensity for being poor – which is one very strong argument in favour of matrimony.' Thus in her novels, it is not just love, but also money which makes the institution of marriage so important.

In 1801 the family had moved to Bath, where she was very unhappy. To make matters worse, in 1805 her father died, leaving his widow, Jane and her only sister Cassandra, also unmarried, even poorer than before. For four years they had to move from house to house, often staying with relatives. (5) ... Finally in 1809 her brother Edward allowed them to live in a house on his estate in Chawton, only a few miles from Steventon where she had grown up. Here she was much happier, despite being the poor relation, dependent on charity. She not only revised her earlier novels but was able to write new ones, using her experiences to satirize and make fun of the social inequalities she saw around her. At last in 1811, *Sense and Sensibility*, (6) ... was the first of her novels to be published.

In 1816, Jane Austen fell ill with a disease of the kidneys. She died on July 18, 1817, in the arms of her sister, Cassandra. She was only 41.

Jane Austen, Hollywood star

The influence of cinema and television has led to worldwide fame for this quiet-living spinster with a sense of fun. People see the movie and then read the book. Not everyone is pleased by this. Winifred Wilson, member of the Jane Austen Society, says, 'These screen adaptations should have kept closer to the text. **They are too heavy on romance and too light on satire.** (7) ...' However, the actress Emma Thompson, who adapted *Sense and Sensibility* for the cinema, won't accept this. She says her screenplay is full of satire, and deals with the relationship between love and money. She went to Jane Austen's grave in Winchester Cathedral to say thank you for the Hollywood Oscar she won for the film. As she said at the Oscar ceremony in Los Angeles, 'I do hope Jane knows how big she is in Uruguay.'

Comprehension check

Work in small groups and discuss the answers.

1 What significance do the following names have in relation to Jane Austen?

Steventon – *the village where Jane was born.*

Chawton	Cassandra
The BBC	Nigel Nicolson
The Internet	P D James
Iceland	John le Carré
Bath	Tom Lefroy
Devon	Winifred Wilson
Uruguay	Emma Thompson
Winchester Cathedral	*Emma*
Edward	Oscar

2 What do these numbers in the text refer to?

41 18 (x3) four (x3) 648.65 200 (x2) eight 12
1802 1805 1811

3 Explain the lines in the text in bold in your own words.

What do you think?

– Do you think Jane Austen had a happy life, or do you feel sorry for her?
– Do you think she would have enjoyed the fame she has today?
– In what ways have the lives of women changed since Jane Austen's time?

● VOCABULARY AND PRONUNCIATION

Making sentences stronger

1 Adverbs and adjectives that go together

1 Look at the adjectives in the box. Find some with similar meanings. Which adjectives go with which of the adverbs on the left? Why?

very / absolutely	good bad big starving valuable silly disgusting fabulous funny interesting incredible pleased exhausted delighted clever priceless dirty beautiful hilarious tired ridiculous awful freezing hungry brilliant frightened fascinating terrified surprising huge right filthy fantastic gorgeous cold

2 The adverb *quite* differs in meaning in these two sentences.

*You're **quite right**.*
*The film is **quite good**.*

In which sentence does *quite* mean *a bit*? In which does it mean *absolutely*?
Give some more examples with the adjectives in the box. What is the rule?

3 **T 8.4** Listen to the short dialogues and complete the gaps.

A That film was _____ _____, wasn't it?

B _____? It was _____ _____!

A You must have been _____ _____ when you passed your exam.

B _____? I was_____ _____!

Make similar short dialogues using adjectives from the box. You could talk about films, books, the weather, holidays, sports, people you know, yourself. Pay particular attention to practising the stress and intonation.

2 Adverbs and verbs that go together

1 Certain intensifying adverbs and verbs often go together. Sometimes there is a logical link. Which verbs in **A** can go with the adverbs in **B**?

A	B
agree	badly
advise	convincingly
behave	distinctly
believe	fully
consider	seriously
forget	sincerely
lie	strongly
recommend	totally
remember	tragically
die	
understand	

2 Underline the correct adverb.

a I *totally/fully* forgot my grandmother's birthday.
b He lied so *convincingly/sincerely* that I *totally/strongly* believed him.
c They *strongly/seriously* advised us to book the tickets in advance.
d I *distinctly/fully* remember packing the sun cream.
e Mozart *tragically/seriously* died when he was still quite young.
f I can't *distinctly/fully* understand what you mean.
g I *absolutely/strongly* adore chocolate ice-cream.
h She is *sincerely/seriously* considering giving up her job.

3 The Oscar ceremony

1 Replace each word underlined with a stronger adjective or adverb.

'I am <u>quite pleased</u> to receive this award. I am <u>very</u> grateful to all those <u>nice</u> people who voted for me. 'Kisses and Dreams' was an <u>interesting</u> movie to work on from start to finish. And I thank all those <u>clever</u> and talented people involved in the making of this <u>very good</u> film. Nobody could have <u>really</u> known that it would be such a <u>big</u> success, especially those who told us at the start that the plot was boring and <u>silly</u>. They have now been proved <u>very</u> wrong. My particular thanks go to Marius Aherne my <u>good</u> director; Julietta Brioche my <u>beautiful</u> co-star; Roger Sims for writing such a <u>funny</u> and <u>exciting</u> story. I <u>really</u> adore you all.'

2 **T 8.5** Listen to the sample answer and compare your choice of adjectives and adverbs.

● LISTENING AND WRITING

The greatest superstar of all!

Pre-listening task

1 Look at the posters advertising some musicals. Have you heard of any of them? Who wrote them?

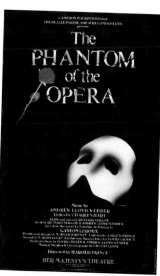

2 T 8.6 Listen to some song extracts. Do you know which of the musicals above they are from?

3 What is the meaning of the words underlined?

a *It wasn't just a successful show, it was a smash hit.*

b *I wasn't just interested, I was absolutely intrigued.*

c *They didn't just criticize it, they hammered it!*

d *You're not allowed to talk about it. It's a taboo subject.*

Listening

Work in pairs or small groups.

Part one *The writer*

You will hear an interview with Tim Rice, who wrote the lyrics for *Jesus Christ Superstar*. It was first performed in the 1970s, but has been performed many times since. Andrew Lloyd Webber composed the music.

1 Discuss the following before you listen.

a What are some of the main events in the life of Jesus Christ? Who were some of the main characters in his life?

b Why do you think Tim Rice and Andrew Lloyd Webber chose to write a musical about Jesus Christ?

c Name some famous people that you would call 'superstars'. Why do you think Rice and Lloyd Webber called Jesus Christ a 'superstar'?

d Why do you think some people protested about the musical?

2 T 8.7 Listen to the first part. What does Tim Rice say about the questions in 1 above?

3 Are these sentences true or false? Correct the false ones.

a There haven't been many versions of the story of Jesus.

b At first they wanted to write about Judas Iscariot.

c They always knew it would be a success.

d The record was an immediate success in America.

e He saw a baby being christened with the name Jesus Christ Superstar.

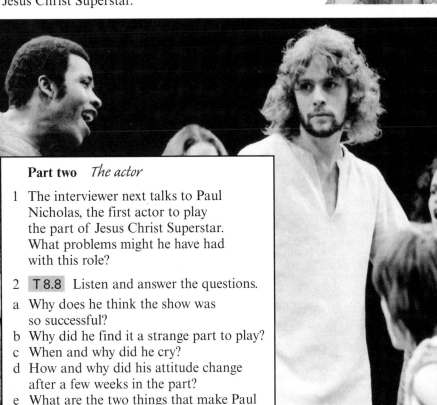

Part two *The actor*

1 The interviewer next talks to Paul Nicholas, the first actor to play the part of Jesus Christ Superstar. What problems might he have had with this role?

2 T 8.8 Listen and answer the questions.

a Why does he think the show was so successful?

b Why did he find it a strange part to play?

c When and why did he cry?

d How and why did his attitude change after a few weeks in the part?

e What are the two things that make Paul Nicholas and the interviewer laugh?

f What is the interviewer's final question? What is Paul's answer?

Writing

A letter from a fan

1 Work in groups. Discuss the following questions. Which famous people do you admire? What do they do? Have you ever belonged to a fan club? Have you ever written a fan letter to anyone who you admire?

2 Read the fan letter written to an actor called Zubin Varla, who played the role of Judas Iscariot in *Jesus Christ Superstar*. What is the aim of each paragraph? Discuss possible endings for each one.

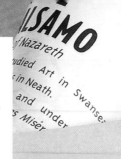

77 Buttermere Rd
High Wycombe
Bucks
March 1st

Dear Zubin
    Last weekend my sister and I saw you (for a second time) in your show Jesus Christ Superstar. It was a magical evening and I felt that I just had to write and tell you...

    Your voice is truly spectacular, really strong and powerful. I think Judas is an extremely difficult part because everybody knows he is a traitor, and they hate him. But you portrayed him in such a way, and with such passion, that I think we began to understand his confused feelings. The other members of the cast...

    I hope you don't mind me writing to you. I expect you get loads of fan letters. I was wondering if you had a fan club of any sort that I could write to. It would be great to find out more about you. I am sixteen and hope to be in a musical when I am older. I go to dance and drama school four times a week. We put on shows every summer, and my teacher says...

    Thank you again for a wonderful evening. If you have time, I would be very grateful if...

        Good luck in your future career.
            Love
                Joanna Jackson

PS We're coming to see the show again next week. It would be great if...

3 Write a fan letter to someone who you admire.

PostScript

Exaggeration and understatement

1 Which nationalities have the reputation for being passionate, spontaneous, and temperamental?
Which nationalities are more controlled and reserved?

2 Which of these declarations of love are exaggerated?
Which are understated?

> I quite like you, you know. D'you think you might get to like me?

> My whole being yearns and burns for you.

> You're a dear old thing, and I'm really rather fond of you.

> I worship the ground you walk on.

> My heart aches to be near you.

3 Match a line in **A** with a line in **B**. Use your dictionary to look up new words.

a ☐ b ☐ c ☐ d ☐ e ☐ f ☐ g ☐ h ☐ i ☐ j ☐ k ☐ l ☐ m ☐

A	B
a I'm starving. I could eat a horse.	1 Yes, it was a nice little break, but all good things must come to an end.
b I'm absolutely dying for a drink.	2 You're not kidding. He's as thick as two short planks.
c His family are pretty well off, aren't they?	3 Yes, my throat's a bit dry, I must say.
d You must have hit the roof when she told you she'd crashed your car.	4 What! He was totally smashed out of his brain!
e I think Tony was a bit tipsy last night.	5 What? That little thing wouldn't hurt a fly!
f I can't stand the sight of him.	6 I know. It *is* a bit wet, but we mustn't grumble, must we?
g He isn't very bright, is he?	7 I'll say. We had to fight our way through millions of people to get to the drinks.
h Look at the weather! It's vile again.	8 OK. I feel a bit out of breath, too.
i What a fantastic holiday!	9 Well, yes, I was a bit upset.
j I'm knackered. Can we stop for a rest?	10 I suppose it did take rather a long time to get here.
k He invited quite a few friends to his party.	11 You can say that again. They're absolutely loaded!
l Well, that journey was absolute hell!	12 I must admit, I'm not too keen on him, either.
m They've got this huge great dog called Wizzer. I'm terrified of it.	13 Yes, I'm a little peckish, too.

Which lines are examples of exaggeration? Which are understatements?

4 **T 8.9** Listen and check your answers. In pairs, practise the dialogues.

Nothing but the truth

Questions and negatives
Being polite

---

1 Make the sentences negative. Sometimes there is more than one possibility.

a I agree with you.
b I think you're right.
c I told her to go home.
d We had lunch at 12.00.
e I've already done my homework.
f You must get a visa.
g The postman has always got something for me.
h (Who wants an ice-cream?) Me.

2 Write the missing questions.

a '_____ you _____?'
   'Jazz, and rock 'n' roll.'

b '_____ you _____ cinema?'
   'About once a fortnight.'

c '_____ she _____?'
   'She's quite tall, with red hair. She's very nice.'

d '_____?'
   'Christopher Columbus.'

e 'I had a long chat with Helen yesterday.'
   '_____ talk _____?'
   'Oh, this and that.'

LANGUAGE IN CONTEXT

Questions and negatives

1 Think of some lies that these people might tell.

> a young boy to his mother   a car salesman   a politician
> a student to the teacher   an estate agent

2 The people in the cartoons are all lying. Why are they lying? What's the truth?

T 9.1 Listen to the truth. Did you guess why they were lying?

3 Match a question to a cartoon. Put a number 1–7 next to each question. Answer the questions.

a ☐ Who wants to speak to me?

b ☐ How is he *really*?

c ☐ I wonder why she doesn't like him.

d ☐ Who's she going out with?

e ☐ What happened last night?

f ☐ What did she buy it for?

g ☐ What's his room-mate like?

● **Grammar questions**

In the questions in Exercise 3, find …

… questions without an auxiliary verb.

… an indirect question.

… questions with a preposition at the end.

… a question that asks for a general description of someone.

… a question that asks about someone's health.

… another way of asking *Why?*

I really like your new dress. It suits you.   3

I'm afraid Miss Jones is out of the office at the moment. Can I take a message?   7

PRACTICE BANK

1 General knowledge quiz

1 Work in pairs.
Your teacher will give you a quiz.
You don't have the same information.
Ask and answer questions.

Example

Student A
Christopher Columbus discovered America in … (When?)
Pablo Picasso, the Spanish artist, painted *Guernica* in … (When?)

Student B
Christopher Columbus discovered America in 1492.
… (Who?) painted the picture *Guernica* in 1937.

> When did Christopher Columbus discover America?
>
> In 1492.
>
> Who painted *Guernica*?
>
> Picasso.
>
> When did he paint it?
>
> In 1937.

2 Make some comments about the answers in the quiz. Some of your sentences might be indirect questions.

Examples
I didn't know | *who wrote 'Dracula'.*
I already knew |
I wonder what the Centennial Exposition in Paris was all about.
I didn't know that Einstein campaigned for nuclear disarmament.

2 Short questions

1 We can answer a statement by asking for more information. These questions can be very short.

Examples
'I went out for a meal last night.' **'Who with?'**
'Tell me a story.' **'What about?'**

Write short questions with a preposition to answer these statements.

a She gave away all her money.
b Can I have a word with you, please?
c I danced all night.
d I need £5,000 urgently.
e Peter's writing a book.
f I got a lovely present today.
g I bought a birthday card today.
h Sh! I'm thinking!
i Do you think you could give me a lift?
j Can you clean the sink, please?

2 Make the short questions into longer ones. Sometimes you need to change the sentences.

Example
Who did you go out for a meal with?
What do you want me to tell you a story about?

T9.2 Listen and check your answers.

3 Vegetarians don't eat meat

1 **T 9.3** Read and listen to this story. There are lots of contradictions in it. Find them.

Example
He's a vegetarian, so he doesn't eat meat. Why was he eating a hot dog?

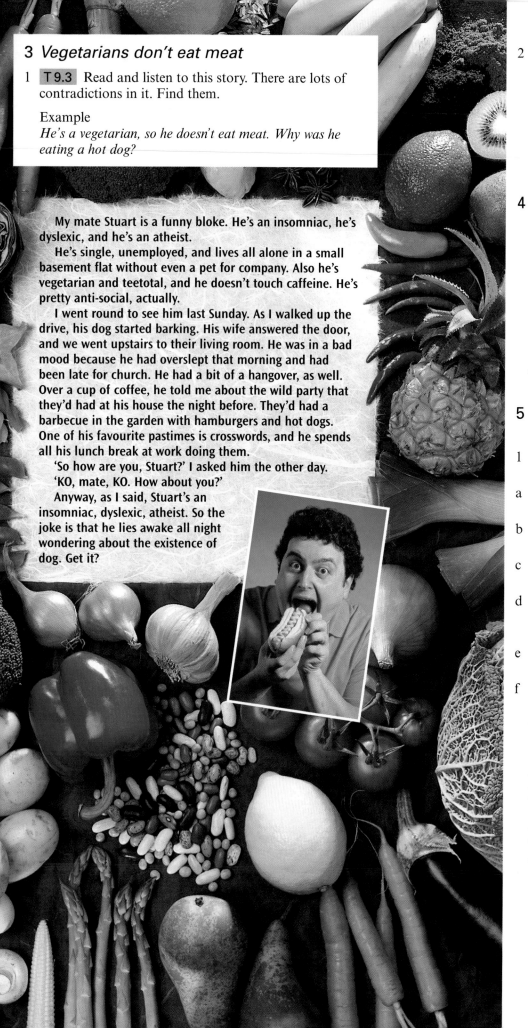

My mate Stuart is a funny bloke. He's an insomniac, he's dyslexic, and he's an atheist.

He's single, unemployed, and lives all alone in a small basement flat without even a pet for company. Also he's vegetarian and teetotal, and he doesn't touch caffeine. He's pretty anti-social, actually.

I went round to see him last Sunday. As I walked up the drive, his dog started barking. His wife answered the door, and we went upstairs to their living room. He was in a bad mood because he had overslept that morning and had been late for church. He had a bit of a hangover, as well. Over a cup of coffee, he told me about the wild party that they'd had at his house the night before. They'd had a barbecue in the garden with hamburgers and hot dogs. One of his favourite pastimes is crosswords, and he spends all his lunch break at work doing them.

'So how are you, Stuart?' I asked him the other day.

'KO, mate, KO. How about you?'

Anyway, as I said, Stuart's an insomniac, dyslexic, atheist. So the joke is that he lies awake all night wondering about the existence of dog. Get it?

---

2 Make a negative sentence about these people. Use your dictionary.

> agnostics   vegans
> claustrophobics
> agoraphobics   workaholics
> animal rights campaigners
> traditionalists

4 Who is it?

Describe someone in the room, using only negative sentences. Can the others guess who it is?

> She can't cook.

> She didn't pass the test last week.

> She never arrives on time.

5 Negative questions and pronunciation

1 **T 9.4** Read and listen to these questions.

a Do you like seafood?
   Yes, I do.

b Don't you like tea or coffee?
   No, I don't.

c Have you ever been to Russia?
   No, I haven't.

d Haven't you done your homework yet?
   Yes, I have.

e Can you type?
   No, I can't.

f Can't you swim?
   Yes, of course I can!

Which questions express the attitude of the speaker?
How does the speaker feel in these questions?
In questions d and f, does *Yes* mean *Yes, you are right. I haven't/I can't?*
Or does it mean *You are wrong. I **have** done it/I **can** do it?*

2 **T 9.5** Listen to the intonation and the contracted forms of the negative questions. Practise saying the questions.

> Don't you ...   Can't they ...   Aren't you ...
> Hasn't she ever ...   Isn't that ...   Haven't I ...
> Hasn't the postman ...   Weren't you ...
> Didn't you ...

3 In pairs, ask and answer negative questions. Ask about these things. Remember! The person who asks the questions must sound surprised.

have got a dictionary/boyfriend/girlfriend/ computer at home

like pizza/learning English/parties

have ever been to a disco/abroad

come to school yesterday/have anything to eat yesterday

can cook/dance/play the piano

LANGUAGE REVIEW

Questions

Notice these question forms.

1 *How* + adjective/adverb

How | **big**   *is your car?*
         | **often** *do you come here?*

2 *What/which* + noun

What films *have you seen recently?*
Which newspaper *do you read?*

3 Prepositions usually go at the end of questions.

*Who did she go out **with**?*
*What did you say that **for**?*

4 There is no inversion (and no *do/does/did*) in subject questions.

Who broke *the window?*
What happens *if I press this button?*

5 There is no inversion (and no *do/does/did*) in indirect questions.

*I don't know when the party **starts**.*
*Could you tell me where the station **is**?*

Negatives

Notice how the negative is formed in these sentences.

She | **hasn't** *got* | *any money.*
      | **doesn't** *have* |

*She told me **not to lose** her book.*
*I **don't think** it's a good idea.*
*We **never** go **anywhere** interesting.*
*'Who broke the window?' '**Not me**.'*

Negative questions

Negative questions usually express the speaker's surprise about a negative situation.

***Haven't** you **had** breakfast yet? It's 10 o'clock.*
***Can't** you **swim**? I thought everyone could swim.*
*You haven't eaten a thing. **Didn't** you **like** it?*

📖 **Grammar Reference: page 140.**

● READING

Mysteries of the universe

Pre-reading task

As you go through your day, do you ever ask yourself any of these questions?

- Why are we here?
- Why are people different?
- When I lose things, where do they go?
- Is the person sitting next to me a time traveller?
- Why did the dinosaurs disappear?
- Is there life on another planet?
- How did the world begin, and how will it end?
- What do animals think about?
- Will we ever find a cure for all disease?

Look at the ten paragraph headings in the reading text on pages 92-3. Which of these topics will be discussed?

Reading

1 Read the texts and answer the questions.

a Why is it most likely that there is life on another planet?
Will alien life forms look like us?

b What do comets consist of?

c Why is it hard to find a cure for colds?

d What three things came into existence with the Big Bang?
What happened *before* it?

e Why could genetics explain left-handedness? What is the reason against this explanation?

f What do our body and brain do while we're asleep?

g When do we yawn?
What happens when we yawn?

h According to the laws of physics, is it possible to travel in time?
What are scientists worried about?

i What are the two possibilities for the future of the universe?

j What explanations are given for the disappearance of socks?

2 Here are the last sentences from some of the texts. Which text do they belong to?

a Meanwhile, the only thing to do is to rest in bed for a few days.

b But people sharing the same experience, such as students in a boring lecture, may start to imitate each other without realizing it.

c And if this is the case, then they've always been with us!

d However, the wisdom of this training is questionable.

e This suggests that we need dreams as a sort of escape from reality.

f It's a long shot, but imagine the implications if they find what they're looking for!

g If there was a beginning, does that mean there will be an end?

3 What do these numbers refer to in the texts?

50	zero	1.4 billion billion	1929
a few billion	9 to 12 billion		
10 per cent	a third		
billions of years from now	decades		

Mysteries

Here is a list of the top ten mysteries of the universe. What is the answer to these puzzles that have plagued human beings for thousands of years? The answer is 'Nobody knows'.

1 Are we alone in the universe?

Probably not. Just the size of the universe makes it unlikely. Alien life forms might not be too far away, either. This year American astronomers discovered a planet capable of sustaining life just 50 light-years away.

But alien life almost certainly won't be like us. Biochemists have calculated that the chances of the chemical combinations necessary to produce life are minute. The possibility that alien life forms will resemble us is zero. NASA is planning a huge deep-space telescope to search for signs of alien life.

2 Where do the oceans come from?

While the world's seas and oceans have been home to life for over three billion years, the origin of the 1.4 billion billion tonnes of water that they collectively contain remains a mystery. It seems to have condensed out of the early earth's atmosphere, but how it got there in the first place isn't known.

One possible theory is that it was dropped on our planet by comets. These gigantic chunks of frozen vapour and dust are rich in water. According to some scientists, satellite pictures have shown that tiny comets continue to hit the earth, topping up our oceans all the time.

3 WILL THERE EVER BE A CURE FOR THE COMMON COLD?

Perhaps, but not yet. The big challenge facing scientists trying to rid mankind of this misery is finding a drug that can combat the huge and ever-changing variety of cold viruses. Researchers are looking for features that all such viruses share. Whichever drug company comes up with something is guaranteed to make a fortune.

4 How old is the universe?

The date of the Big Bang has caused astronomers trouble since they discovered that the universe was expanding in 1929. At the time, measurements of the rate of expansion suggested an age of a few billion years. Latest figures, using the Hubble Space Telescope, suggest nine to twelve billion years.

But what happened before the Big Bang? No one knows. According to current theories of the birth of the universe, not only matter but also space and time came into being with the Big Bang. If correct, these theories imply that there was no 'before' the Big Bang. However, this proposition raises many fundamental questions.

of the universe

5 Why are some people left-handed?

About 10 per cent of the population is left-handed, and it seems to run in families. The cause, therefore, seems obvious: genetics. However, identical twins, who have identical genetic blueprints, aren't necessarily both left-handed or right-handed. This would appear to disprove the theory that being left-handed is inherited.

Even at birth most babies tend to move one arm, usually the right, more than the other. Some scientists believe that the use of left hand or right hand is a result of the baby's environment. Most children can be trained to use and to prefer the right hand for any activity.

6 WHY DO WE SLEEP?

On average we spend a third of our lives sleeping, but no one really knows why. The most popular theory is that sleeping gives the body and brain a chance to recover from the stresses of the day. But beyond this vague statement, we don't know what this recuperation consists of. Warm-blooded species, including humans, birds, and mammals, seem to need more sleep than cold-blooded creatures such as fish and reptiles, so there is a possibility that we sleep in order to save energy. Sleep deprivation produces hallucinations.

7 WHY IS YAWNING INFECTIOUS?

This is a tough one. No one even knows what purpose yawning serves at all. But we do know that fatigue, boredom, and anxiety can trigger off a yawn.

Like crying and laughing, yawning is a variant of normal breathing. Yawning is a reflex action, not under conscious control. The mouth opens wide and you take a longer, deeper breath than usual. Yawning momentarily raises the heart rate, forcing more blood to the brain. One theory is that yawning makes you more alert by making you breathe in more.

Yawning isn't infectious in the clinical sense of the word.

8 Does nature allow time travel?

Amazingly, there is nothing in the known laws of physics to prevent us from zooming off into the past or future. Exactly how one would build a time-machine is anyone's guess, but many scientists have a bigger worry – paradoxes such as killing your mother before she gave birth to you. Maybe Nature has a clever way of getting round these. Or maybe there's an as yet undiscovered barrier to time travel. But just think! If at any time in the future time travel becomes possible, then time travellers are with us now!

9 HOW WILL THE UNIVERSE END?

This depends on how much matter exists in the cosmos. If it exceeds the so-called critical density, gravity will bring the current cosmic expansion to a halt and trigger a contraction or implosion billions of years from now. Alternatively, the universe may expand for ever. After decades of research, astronomers still don't know precisely how much matter exists in the universe, and so cannot predict accurately how the universe will end. The consensus, however, is that the cosmos will expand for ever.

10 Where do all the odd socks go to?

Open any sock drawer and you'll find odd socks. Theories about what happens to them range from disappearing down black holes in the universe to being eaten by washing machines. Another explanation is that in every house there lurks a place where all the missing things live ...

What do you think?

Which mysteries do you find the most interesting? What mysteries would you like answered?

Why do I never have enough money?
What will life be like in 2050?
Why is my bus never on time?

VOCABULARY

Making connections in texts

1 Antonyms and synonyms often occur in texts. Which are the antonyms and synonyms in these sentences?

If there was a beginning, does that mean there will be an end?
… gravity will bring the current cosmic expansion to a halt and trigger a contraction …
… astronomers still don't know precisely how much matter exists in the universe, and so cannot predict accurately …

2 Write in antonyms for these words.

Word	Antonym
huge	
happiness	
guilty	
criticize	
reward	
cruelty	
dangerous	
succeed	
genuine	
improve	
admit	
permanent	
profit	
brave	
attack	
crazy	

3 What's the opposite of … ?

a tough question	fair hair
tough meat	a fair decision
rich food	a sweet apple
a rich person	sweet wine
a strong man	a hard exam
a strong taste	a hard mattress
clear instructions	a free man
a clear sky	a free seat

4 There can be near antonyms in a text.
*Peter said he **understood** the lecture, but it **didn't make any sense** to me at all.*
The word class can change, for example from adjective to noun.
*At first they thought the picture was **genuine**, but then it was found to be **a fake**.*

5 Complete the sentences with words from the box. Put the words in the correct form.

| improve safe casualty mystery solve succeed criticize fail |
| survive good fun encourage a disaster get worse danger |

a He's a very _____ businessman, but he has always _____ to find happiness.

b I thought the party would be _____, but it was _____ from start to finish. I didn't know anyone and I didn't speak to anyone.

c I'm pleased to say that there have been many _____ in your behaviour this term, but unfortunately your work _____.

d 'Were there many _____ in the accident?' 'No, it was a miracle. Everyone _____.'

e I tried to fix my computer, but the instructions were a total _____ to me. Fortunately, my son _____ the problem in five seconds.

f Bungee jumping sounds _____, but it's _____ enough if you're careful.

g Our teacher is strict, but fair. He can be very _____ if we make silly mistakes, but he does give us lots of _____ if we've tried hard.

6 What is the effect of using antonyms in these sentences?

*'Jenny's **thick**, isn't she?' 'Well, she isn't very **bright**, it's true.'*
*'What **lousy** weather!' 'No, it's not very **nice**, is it?'*

In pairs, write similar dialogues. How could you describe the following both honestly and tactfully?

| a terrible dinner party   an awful holiday   an unsuccessful meeting |
| an uncomfortable hotel   a terrible football match   a difficult exam |

● LISTENING AND SPEAKING

Saying 'I won't'

Pre-listening task

1 When did you last go to a wedding? Whose was it? Where was it? What happened?

2 What do you need to do if you plan to get married? What preparations are necessary for the actual wedding day? Write a list and then compare it with a partner's.

3 Look at the photos of Elizabeth, George, and Nicole. They each have a story about a wedding. The cartoons tell part of their story. What can you see? Discuss what you think has happened.

Elizabeth

George

Nicole

Listening

1 **T 9.6** Read and listen to the introduction to a radio programme.

This is Radio 4. This week in File on Life **Saying 'I won't'** or **What stopped the wedding?**

The photographer may be booked, the cake may be iced, and the dress may fit perfectly, but suddenly it's all off. What stops the wedding and forces one half of the happy couple into saying 'I won't'? Listen to the stories of Elizabeth, George, and Nicole.

2 Look at the cartoons below. What do you think stopped the weddings of Elizabeth, George, and Nicole?

3 Listen to the rest of the programme. Are your ideas correct? What exactly do the cartoons above and below illustrate?

Comprehension check

Answer the questions about each of the stories.

1 Who was he/she going to get married to?

2 Why didn't he/she get married?

3 Who called off the wedding in each case?

4 Which other people are mentioned? What part do they play in the stories?

5 Who said these lines? What are they referring to?

a *He was like my brother.*
b *... he thrust a piece of paper in my hand and ran.*
c *... it was a really smashing day.*
d *Come on, it's just nerves.*
e *... she couldn't fill the forms in, she had a panic attack.*
f *It was such a relief, it was like a cork coming out of a bottle, it all just poured out.*
g *All I can remember is dancing non-stop.*
h *... I just can't do it, I can't face it.*
i *We had so much in common.*

6 Imagine you are these people.
Elizabeth's mother (story 1)
Vicky (story 2)
A wedding guest (story 3)

Retell each story from that person's point of view.

The song

1 **T 9.7** Listen to the whole song. Can you remember any of the words?

2 Turn to page 131. Read the words and listen to the song.

● WRITING

Joining sentences

1 Sentences can be joined using conjunctions. Conjunctions introduce clauses such as time, reason, result, purpose, condition, and contrast.

Time	Reason	Result	Purpose	Condition	Contrast
when(ever) while as (soon as) until after since	because as since so	so ... that such ... that	so that in case	if unless as long as	but although even though

Your teacher will give you an exercise on conjunctions.

2 Some adverbs express the speaker's attitude to what is being said.

What a terrible journey! **Anyway**, *you're here now, so come on in!*
Anyway means *I want to change the subject.*
Actually, *my name's Peter, not Tom.*
I'm going out tonight, **actually***. Sorry I can't help.*

Actually is used to make what you're saying softer, especially if you're correcting someone, disagreeing, or complaining.

3 Here is a witness's account of a crime. Choose the best expressions to join the sentences.

It happened at about 6.00 yesterday evening, **(a) while/after** I was coming home from work. **(b) Because/Whenever** I can, I walk to work **(c) if not/except when** it's raining, **(d) because/so that** I like the exercise. **(e) In fact/Anyway**, I was coming down Station Road, and **(f) just as/since** I was walking past number 38, I heard a noise. It was **(g) so/such** a loud noise that I stopped. It sounded **(h) as/as if** a chest of drawers had been knocked over. I know that a lot of old people live alone on this street, so **(i) naturally/surely** I was a little concerned. **(j) Firstly/At first**, I didn't know what to do. I went up to the front door and listened **(k) for see/to see** if I could hear anything. **(l) Of course/In fact**, the front door was ajar, **(m) so/then** I pushed the door and went in. It was **(n) so/such** dark that I couldn't see anything, **(o) but/although** my eyes soon got used to it.

I went into the dining room, and there on the floor was the body of an old man. He had been attacked. **(p) Even though/As soon as** I saw him, I was scared **(q) in case/unless** the burglar was **(r) still/always** in the house. I knelt down to feel his pulse.

(s) However/Although he had been badly beaten up, he was still alive, **(t) fortunately/obviously**. I went to look for a damp cloth **(u) because/so that** I could bathe his wounds, then found his phone and dialled 999. I stayed with him **(v) until/unless** the ambulance arrived, and **(w) when/by** the time the police came, he had woken up and was talking about the attack. **(x) Apparently/Actually**, he had been working in his garden when a man had jumped on him. He didn't see him, and he didn't hear him, **(y) as well/either**.

The old man is now in hospital, and **(z) as soon as/as long as** he takes things easy, he should make a complete recovery.

4 Write a description of a crime or accident through the eyes of a witness. Write about 350 words.

PostScript

Being polite

1 What are 'white lies'? What would you say in these situations?

- You're having a meal with your host family. You've forced yourself to eat something you really don't like, when your host says, 'You must have some more!'
- A friend has just had a baby who you think looks like any other new-born baby. 'Isn't he absolutely gorgeous?' she coos. What do you say?

2 **T 9.8** Listen to the pairs of dialogues. One is more polite than the other. Say which one is more polite, and why.
In pairs, look at the tapescripts and practise the dialogues.

3 Make these requests more polite. Use the expressions below.

Give me a lift.   What's the time?
Lend me your pen.   Where is there a phone?
Help me find my glasses.   When do we have lunch?

> *Could you … ?*   *Do you think you could … ?*
> *Would you mind … ?*   *Do you know … ?*
> *I wonder if you could … ?* *Do you happen to know … ?*

4 **T 9.9** Listen to the requests and invitations, and refuse them politely. Use one of these expressions.

> That's very kind of you, but …   I'd love to, but …
> I'm terribly sorry. I'm afraid I …
> Believe me, I would if I could, but …

T 9.10 Listen and compare your answers.

5 **T 9.11** You are going to a dinner party in London. Your name is Pat. Listen to the conversation, and when you hear a *Ping!* you must speak! You have brought some flowers for your hosts.

10 Things ain't what they used to be!

Expressing habit
Time expressions

---

1 Read the sentences and <u>underline</u> those words which express habit and frequency.

a I very rarely go to church.
b My Aunt Dora used to go to church regularly.
c I usually watch my son's football matches.
d My father used to watch me playing football.
e I have to take this medicine regularly.
f We occasionally visit my uncle in Scotland.
g We used to stay with my grandparents in the country.
h We'd go skating on the village pond.

i She hardly ever writes home but she often phones.
j She'll frequently e-mail us.
k My computer's *always* breaking down.

Which of the sentences express present habit? Which express past habit?

2 How often do you think the actions in Exercise 1 happen or happened? Use the time expressions in the boxes.

Examples
My children go to the dentist <u>regularly</u>.
We <u>used to</u> walk in the park.

They go to the dentist twice a year.
We used to walk/walked in the park every Sunday.

once twice three times	a day a week a fortnight a month a year	every	day year weekend Christmas Sunday

LANGUAGE IN CONTEXT

Past and present habit

1 Look at the photograph and read about a lady called Rosemary Sage. Discuss with a partner which words could complete the gaps.

LIVING HISTORY

Rosemary Sage is 100 years old. She lives in the village of Hambledon, Surrey. Many people (a) _____ daily from Hambledon to work in London. Rosemary has only been to London once in her life, when she went to the zoo sixty years ago! Her daily routine goes back to a time before there were any commuters in the village. It never varies. At the start of each day she (b) _____ wood for the fire, on which she (c) _____ a large kettle of water. Then she (d) _____ some of the water to her wash-house in the garden and she (e) _____ . Next she (f) _____ a cup of tea. She has no means of heating or cooking apart from the open fire. Her home is like a working museum, and her clear memory is a precious source of knowledge of old country ways. She (g) _____ stories of when she was young. In those days the Lord and Lady of the Manor (h) _____ all

2 The words below are the actual words which appeared in the original newspaper article. Put them into the correct gaps in the text.

> gathers and chops   commute
> 'll boil   would freeze over
> used to own   'll get washed
> 'll make herself   'll carry
> 'm used to   'd go skating
> 's always telling   'd spend
> rented   get used to

T 10.1 Listen and check your answers.

3 Discuss the ways in which your ideas for filling the gaps differed from the actual words and verb forms used.

the cottages and they (i) _____ them to the villagers for 2s 9d (14p) a week. Every winter the village pond (j) _____ and she (k) _____ with her six brothers and sisters. Every summer they (l) _____ one day at the seaside. Other than that and her one trip to London, she has hardly ever left the village. She is perfectly content with her life. She has no bath, no fridge, and no telephone. 'I could never (m) _____ such 'modern' appliances at my age,' she says. 'I (n) _____ the old ways. I'm far too old to change.'

Grammar questions

– In which of the following sentences can *used to* be used? In which can *would* be used? In which can neither be used? Why?

We lived in London when I was a child.
We went to the park every Sunday.
We went to the zoo last Sunday.

– Which of the pairs of sentences below express the speaker's attitude? What *is* the attitude?

a	Our cat plays Our cat'll play	with a ball of string for hours.
b	Our cat is **always** playing Our cat **will** play	on the kitchen table.

Put the sentences into the past.

PRACTICE BANK

1 Discussing grammar

Work in pairs. Discuss which sentence in **B** *best* continues the sentence in **A**.

	A	B
a	My grandfather smokes a pipe. He'll sit and smoke it every evening after dinner. He *will* smoke it at the dinner table.	My mother gets really annoyed at this. He always enjoys doing this. It's a habit he's had for over fifty years.
b	We once went skiing in Colorado. We used to go to skiing in Colorado.	We'd fly to Denver and then we'd drive up into the Rockies. We flew to Denver and then we drove up into the Rockies.
c	John usually does the cooking, John used to do the cooking, John's used to doing the cooking, John's getting used to doing the cooking,	because he's been doing it for so many years. but he isn't tonight. but he doesn't any more. but it's taking a long time.
d	It rained on my wedding day. It *would* rain on my wedding day.	Everybody got very wet. This is so typical of the kind of thing that happens to me.
e	He always brings Mel to our parties, He's *always* bringing Mel to our parties,	which is just fine by us. and nobody can stand her! It drives us crazy!

2 Listening and speaking

1 You are going to hear Kathy talking about her first friend, Gillian. Read some information about Gillian and look up any new words in your dictionary. Do you think they are still friends?

My First Friend

a *She used to live up the road in a big white house.*
b *We used to go to the same school but we never used to see much of each other at school.*
c *Her dad used to have a really good job.*
d *We fought a lot.*
e *We both used to love going to the cinema.*
f *We learned all of the words of the songs.*
g *We'd have these huge rows.*
h *I thought she was spoilt rotten.*
i *She always got four flavours and an ice lolly.*
j *She never shared a thing. She was always bursting into tears.*
k *She once fell off her bike and broke her front teeth.*
l *I used to go on holiday to Blackpool with her and her Auntie Ethel.*

2 **T 10.2** Listen very carefully to all that Kathy says. There are some small differences in each of the sentences. Change them to *exactly* what you hear. Careful! One of the sentences is *not* on the tape. Mark it with a ✗.

3 Go through the sentences a–l with a partner and for each one try to remember some of the extra information you heard. Listen again to check.

4 Prepare a short talk about *either* one of your first friends *or* one of your first teachers. Give it to the rest of the class and answer any questions they may have.

3 Short answers and pronunciation

1 Complete the answers. Use *usually*, *used to*, or a form of *be/get used to*, in the positive and the negative. Add any other necessary words.

Examples
'Do you translate every word when you read?'
'No, but I *used to*.'

'You didn't like your new teacher, did you?'
'No, but we soon *got used to* her.'

a How often do you get homework?
  Well, we _____ twice a week.

b Do you read many books in English?
  Well, yes, I do now, but I _____ .

c Do you find it easy to use your monolingual dictionary?
  I didn't at first, but I soon _____ .

d Do you look up every word that you can't understand?
  Well, I don't now, but I _____ when I was a beginner.

e How can you understand English when it is spoken so quickly?
  Well, I suppose I _____ .

f Did you do much pronunciation practice when you were first learning English?
  Oh, yes we did. We _____ every lesson.

g How do you find using the telephone in English?
  It's not easy, but I think that gradually I _____ .

2 **T 10.3** Listen and check your answers. Practise the questions and answers with a partner. Go through them again and change the answers so that they are true about you.

LANGUAGE REVIEW

Verbs forms expressing habit

Present habit

1 The Present Simple is the most common tense for expressing present habit. It is often used with adverbs of frequency.
*He **usually** travels by train.*

2 *Will* expresses characteristic behaviour. This is how you expect someone or something to behave. It is usually contracted, and not stressed.
*She**'ll spend** hours just staring out of the window.*
*In Canada it**'ll snow** for days without stopping.*

3 The Present Continuous can be used to express an annoying habit with adverbs of frequency such as *always*, *continually*, and *constantly*.
*I**'m always losing** my car keys.*

4 *Will*, when decontracted and stressed, can also express annoying behaviour.
*She **WILL** put on the radio whenever I'm trying to work!*

Past habit

1 *Would* is the past form of *will* above.
*She**'d spend** hours just staring out of the window.*
*She **WOULD** put on the radio whenever I was trying to work!*

2 *Used to* expresses past states and actions.
Used is a verb.
*He **used to be** rich. (= a state)*
*He **used to do** his homework while watching TV.* (= an action)

Would can be used to express a past action, but not a past state.
*He**'d do** his homework while watching TV.*
NOT ~~He'd be~~ …

Be/get used to + noun/-ing

Here, *used* is an adjective. It means *familiar with or accustomed to as a result of experience.*

*I was brought up on a farm, so I**'m used to** hard work.*
*I lived in the country for twenty years, but I**'m slowly getting used to** living in a city.*

📖 **Grammar Reference: page 141.**

● VOCABULARY

Money, money, money!

1 All the words in columns **A** and **B** have something to do with money. Match a word in **A** with its *closest opposite* in **B**. Use your dictionary to check new words.

A	B
generous	waste
spendthrift	second-hand
luxury	well off
brand new	loss
hard up	stingy
deposit (v)	expenditure
save	overdrawn
in the black	penny-pincher
debt	withdraw
tight-fisted	extravagant
income	priceless
worthless	millionaire
beggar	necessity
profit	loan

2 Complete the following sentences, including words from **A** or **B**.

a Tom couldn't afford a brand new car …

b Do you see that vase? We thought it was worthless. I paid only 50p for it in a jumble sale, but …

c I think that nowadays a car is a necessity, but my grandmother says …

d My two daughters are so different. One regularly saves her pocket money, the other …

e Susie's always getting into debt and then she has to go to her father …

f I was so sure my account was in the black, but I've just got an angry letter …

g You'd never believe that he used to be a millionaire, now …

h Ted's so tight-fisted. He's worn the same suit every day for work for 15 years, but his wife …

i Anna's always complaining about being hard up, but compared to me …

j Mr Micawber's advice to his young friend, David Copperfield, in the year 1850:

'Annual _____ £20, annual _____ £19 and six shillings, result happiness.

Annual _____ £20, annual _____ £20 and six pence, result misery.'

3 Would you be happy or miserable if you:
- fell on hard times?
- lived on a shoestring?
- lived in the lap of luxury?
- were living rough?
- couldn't make ends meet?
- were rolling in money?
- had to penny-pinch?
- were made of money?
- were down and out?
- had to tighten your belt?
- had a business that was doing a roaring trade?
- lost a quid and found a fiver?

● READING AND SPEAKING

MONEY MAKES THE WORLD GO ROUND

Work in pairs or small groups.

Pre-reading task

You are going to read about four very different people, and the role that money plays in their lives. Discuss these questions.

1 The texts are about an aristocrat, a divorced mum, a taxman, and a miser. Which of them do you think is wealthy? Who is poor? What attitude do you think each has to money? How do their lifestyles differ?

2 The following words were said by one of the four people. Who said what? There are two statements for each person. Check any new words in your dictionary.

a 'Money's been tight since I split up from my husband four years ago.'

b 'In my job it's possible to become a bit of a social leper.'

c 'I don't believe one should spend what one hasn't got.'

d 'I'll organize an office collection for earthquake victims, but I won't give anything myself.'

e 'I'd baulk at buying a couple of packets of crisps as well.'

f 'Sometimes I'll go wild and buy something just to cheer myself up, but I always regret it.'

g 'We always do our own repairs to the house, or we'll put a bucket out to catch the leaks if we can't.'

h 'People think I've got a fortune stashed away somewhere.'

Reading

1 Read all *four* texts quickly and find out who said what. Were there any surprises? Which of the four is the richest? Who is the poorest?

2 Choose *two* of the texts and read them more carefully. Answer the questions.

a What is his/her job? How much does he/she earn?
b Does he/she get on well with his wife/her husband?
c What does he/she say about clothes and food?
d What else does he/she spend money on?
e Does he/she give any money to charities or good causes?
f In what ways does he/she try to save money?
g Does he/she have any extravagances?
h What do you learn about his/her friends and/or family?

Speaking

1 Find someone who chose different texts from you. Go through the questions together and compare the information.

2 Which people do these words describe? Why?

> thrifty   skinflint   well off   hard up
> privileged   underprivileged

3 Discuss how money (or the lack of it!) affects your life.

PEOPLE AND THEIR MONEY

Who's rich and who's poor these days? Gina Brooks tracks down four people from very different walks of life.

THE ARISTOCRAT

LADY CHRYSSIE COBBOLD, 58, lives in Knebworth House, Hertfordshire, the family home of her husband David, 60, a financier. They have four grown-up children.

'Knebworth House is run as a business but it doesn't make enough money to pay us. I have no regular salary. I never really spend money because I don't have it and I'm not bothered about clothes. I spend about £2,000 a year on them. There have been moments when we thought we might have to sell the house, but now I think there'll be enough money for the next generation to keep the house, but they won't inherit much more than that.

Money is the only thing my husband and I row about. I'm always worrying about money. I don't believe one should spend what one hasn't got. My husband likes having parties, going to restaurants, having guests for the weekend. In summer we'll have up to 16 people at weekends. They're usually quite good and they'll bring a bottle of wine, but they still have to be fed.

We always do our own repairs to the house or we'll put a bucket out to catch the leaks if we can't. I'll go to any lengths to save money. I'll put up wallpaper, do all the painting, make curtains and upholstery. As a child I used to get only 5p a week pocket money and I'd do anything to get more money. I'd even pick bunches of flowers from our garden and sell them to the local funeral parlour.

If you have a big house, people think you must be well off, but it just isn't true.'

THE DIVORCED MUM

ANGIE CROSS, 27, has four children, aged from 5 to 10. She lives in Frinton-on-Sea in Essex. She gets £585 a month state benefit and also works as a part-time barmaid for £21 a week.

'Money's been tight since I split up from my husband four years ago. The kids always come first, but special occasions for them are rare. They're lucky if we go to McDonald's once a month. All their school uniforms are second-hand. When I was a kid I used to get lots of treats. I'd go riding and I used to have piano lessons. I feel dreadful not being able to give my kids the things I had. Every month I work out exactly what has to be paid and what can wait. I have to be very careful with money, and that doesn't come easily because by nature I'm very extravagant. My biggest extravagance now is a packet of ten cigarettes.

My monthly food bill comes to about £350, and towards the end of the month we have beans on toast three nights out of seven. I usually make the kids a packed lunch for school, but occasionally I don't have enough food to make one, so I tell the kids to have a school dinner and say they've forgotten their dinner money. It's not really telling lies because I'll always pay as soon as I can.

I get very depressed and I frequently sit down and cry. Sometimes I'll go wild and buy something just to cheer myself up, but I always regret it. I once spent £30 on some clothes but I felt really guilty. What I want more than anything else is a holiday and new shoes for the kids. Who knows? I might win the lottery!'

THE TAXMAN

BOB WILDEN, 24, is a tax inspector. He earns £23,558 per annum. His wife, Denise, 20, earns £7,500 as a part-time secretary. They live in Maidenhead, Berkshire. They have no children.

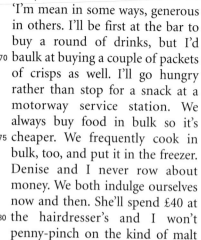

'I'm mean in some ways, generous in others. I'll be first at the bar to buy a round of drinks, but I'd baulk at buying a couple of packets of crisps as well. I'll go hungry rather than stop for a snack at a motorway service station. We always buy food in bulk so it's cheaper. We frequently cook in bulk, too, and put it in the freezer. Denise and I never row about money. We both indulge ourselves now and then. She'll spend £40 at the hairdresser's and I won't penny-pinch on the kind of malt whisky I get. I never spend much on clothes though, probably about £95 at the most. I don't need to look smart to be a taxman.

Denise generally gives £20 a month to animal charities, but she won't donate to beggars wearing £100 trainers. I'll give the real down-and-outs a quid sometimes. My widowed mum is a pensioner and lives alone, so I always make sure that she has enough to eat.

I have four credit cards, but one is never used. A bill for £700 arrived this morning for one of them. It frightened us to death. Occasionally we have to get loans to clear our credit card debts. In my job it's possible to become a bit of a social leper. Some friends are always boasting to me about how they dodge paying tax. I don't like that. I don't like paying tax either, but I'd never dodge it.'

THE MISER

MALCOLM STACEY, 38, is a part-time BBC journalist and author of two books about money. He earns £50,000 per annum. He lives in York with his wife Jo, 32. They have two young children.

'I never buy luxuries and I never buy a round of drinks. When colleagues go out to the pub, I'll stay in the office and say I'm expecting a phone call. I'll never invite people to dinner, but I never feel guilty about accepting their invitations. I know they invite me to have someone interesting to talk to. The meanest thing I've ever done was to go to a wedding without a present. I just took some wrapping paper and a tag saying 'Love from Malcolm' and put it onto the table with the other presents. I got a thank-you letter from the bride. She obviously thought she'd mislaid the present.

People don't believe I can be so stingy. I'll organize an office collection for earthquake victims but I won't give anything myself. I've put a wishing well in the front garden. I would never ask passers-by to throw money in, but I collect it when they do. I hardly ever use my car; we grow our own vegetables and we recycle everything. We never buy new clothes, we get them second-hand from charity shops for about £2 a garment. We can live on £5 a week.

I've always been mean. When I was a child I would never buy flowers for Mum, but I'd give her a bouquet from her own garden. My wife gets embarrassed by my meanness, but we never row about money. People think I've got a fortune stashed away somewhere. I don't care what they think.'

Language work

Hot Verbs (4): come and go

There are many common expressions with the verbs *come* and *go*. These examples come from the texts.

*I'll **go** to any lengths ...*
*The kids always **come** first ...*
*My monthly food bill **comes** to about £350 ...*
*Sometimes I'll **go** wild ...*

Decide which verb fits these sentences.

a Mini-skirts *came/went* into fashion in the 1960s.
b Ugh! The milk's *come/gone* sour!
c I don't feel old, but I'm beginning to *go/come* grey.
d This sweater won't *go/come* in my suitcase. I'll have to carry it.
e Jane and I have *come/gone* to an agreement. I'll shop if she cooks.
f 'It's my dream to meet someone famous.' 'I hope your dream *goes/comes* true.'
g Most of my money *comes/goes* on bills.
h With coffees and VAT, your bill *goes/comes* to £90.
i How did your interview *go/come*?
j Britain *came/went* second in the 100 metres.
k I think I must be *going/coming* mad.
l The time has *come/gone* to make a decision.
m My brother's business *came/went* bankrupt.
n That tie *goes/comes* really well with your jacket.
o Everything will *come/go* right in the end.

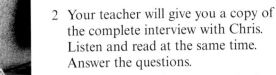

LISTENING

HOMELESSNESS

Pre-listening task

Discuss the questions as a class.

1 Where do people live when they have no home? How do they live?
2 Who are they? How could they have ended up homeless?
3 Do you think politicians are interested in the problem? Why/why not?

Part 1 Listening

T 10.4 Listen to a radio interview with Oliver McGechy, who runs a home for alcoholics and homeless people in Guildford, a wealthy town near London. Answer the questions.

a Why is Oliver particularly suited to running a home for alcoholics and homeless people?
b What is the average lifespan for homeless people in Europe? How is this moving back to Victorian days?
c What is just 'the tip of the iceberg'?
d What is Oliver referring to when he says … ?
'… they've probably lost all of the network which has supported them within society.'
'… they're into a downward spiral …'
'… there's little political gain in supporting homeless people.'
e Who are the people who become homeless?
f What question does Oliver ask the interviewer?

Part 2 Listening and reading

The second person to be interviewed is Chris Caine, aged 33, who is staying in the home that Oliver runs.

1 Chris is a Londoner and speaks with quite a strong London accent. Read the exact transcript of the first part of what he says. Try to work out what he is saying. What differences do you notice from standard English?

> I Chris, can you tell us why it was that you ended up homeless?
> CC Well, I 'ad a house wiv a woman that I … er took on, wiv 'er kids and I 'ad a job'n all, workin' at the Royal Mail Post Office … erm I dunno about … what … er two, two years it was into the relationship and all of a sudden, like, she just wanted out, so … er I tried to patch fings up which really didn't work, yer know, so I ended up going back to the woods, well, yer know where I was before …
> I Back to the woods?
> CC Yeah.
> I How d'you mean? Literally to the woods?
> CC Yeah. I used to live out in the woods.

2 Your teacher will give you a copy of the complete interview with Chris. Listen and read at the same time. Answer the questions.

a How did Chris become homeless?
b What does the interviewer express surprise about?
c Why does Chris feel more at ease living in the woods than in the town?
d Why did he leave the woods? What did he use to do there?
e What jobs has he had?
f What does he miss most about not having a home? Does he enjoy being alone?
g What hurts Chris most of all?
h Where do homeless people sleep?
i Which takes Chris the longest to get used to, being on the road or living with the rest of society?

Part 3 Listening

Listen to the conclusion of the programme. What does Chris say about drink? Do you think that Chris has a good chance of getting a job and a home again?

Discussion

These were the opening words of the interviewer.

'Why is it that, even in the richest countries in the world, there are so many homeless people?'

Which rich countries do you know of where homelessness is a problem? Is there a problem of homelessness in your country? If so, do you know any reasons for it? How do you feel about homeless people? Do you try to help if you can? Why/Why not?

Writing about a period in history

1 Choose a time in the history of your country that interests you and do some research into the kind of lives people used to lead then. Try to find out information about the following topics:

Homes and Food   Health
Pastimes   Education

2 Which period did you choose? Why? Discuss your findings as a class.

3 Read the text about Britain in the time of the Tudors. Check new words in your dictionary. Write in the correct paragraph headings from Exercise 1.

LIFE IN TUDOR BRITAIN

The Tudors ruled Britain from 1485 to 1603. Henry VIII and Elizabeth I were both Tudor monarchs.

➾ 1 _____

Tudor towns were very small and overcrowded. The cobbled streets were narrow, filthy, and very unhealthy. Few people lived to be older than 40, and children often died before they were five. Open sewers carried the filth to the nearest river, rats and flies thrived, spreading diseases such as typhus and plague.

➾ 2 _____

The rich lived in mansions in the countryside. These were very big with up to 150 servants. They had a great many chimneys because so many fires were needed to keep the vast rooms warm, and to cook the food for their huge feasts, which consisted of up to ten courses. They would regularly eat venison, blackbirds, and larks but rarely had potatoes because although explorers such as Sir Walter Raleigh had brought them to Britain, they were not, as yet, grown very frequently by British farmers. Honey was normally used to sweeten food; sugar was only rarely available, but when they did have it, they put it on all their food, including meat! The poor never had sugar or potatoes and seldom ate meat. They would occasionally catch rabbits and fish but most of the time they ate bread and vegetables such as cabbage and turnips.

➾ 3 _____

Poorer children never went to school. Children from better-off families had tutors to teach them reading and French. However, boys were often sent to schools which belonged to the monasteries and there they would learn mainly Latin in classes of up to 60 boys. The school day went from dawn until dusk, and the schoolmasters would frequently beat their pupils.

➾ 4 _____

The rich used to go hunting to kill deer and wild boar for their feasts. They also enjoyed fencing and jousting contests. The poor watched bear fighting and also played a kind of football where they jumped on each other, often breaking their necks and backs. There were some theatres and people enjoyed watching plays, particularly those of a young playwright called William Shakespeare.

PostScript

Time expressions

1 Use your dictionary and check that you understand the meaning of the words underlined in **A**.

A	B
a I've been <u>brushing up</u> my German	in the olden days.
b I <u>came across</u> this old newspaper <u>cutting</u>	all day long.
c We <u>made it</u> to the airport	by Friday at the latest.
d Despite the <u>blizzard</u> our plane took off	some time soon.
e I have to <u>put up with</u> this <u>poky</u> office	many years ago.
f They've promised to fax us the <u>trade figures</u>	lately.
g I'll get <u>in touch</u> with James	Take your time!
h He <u>moans</u> about the weather	It's a waste of time.
i We used to go <u>rambling</u> in the hills	in record time.
j He'll sit in his chair, <u>muttering</u> to himself	for hours upon end.
k Men would often wear <u>tights</u>	the other day.
l You should never <u>gobble</u> your food!	by the end of the week.
m Please <u>drop in</u> to see us again	at the end of the week.
n Don't look up every word.	before long.
	just in time.
	on time.
	for the time being.

2 How many natural-sounding sentences can you make using a line in **A** with time expressions in **B**? Work alone, then check your ideas with a partner.

3 Write your own sentences to illustrate the meaning of each of the expressions in **B**. Then work in small groups and compare your sentences.

4 Compare Tudor Britain with the period you have researched. Are there any similarities? Write a similar piece about your period using the four headings.

11 If only things were different!

Hypothesizing
Moans and groans

Test your grammar

1 Read about Tom's Monday morning blues in column **A**.

'I've got those Monday morning blues!'

A		B
a It's Monday morning.		
b I've overslept.		it had.
c My alarm didn't go off.		there was.
d I drank too much last night.		I could.
e I feel sick.	**I wish**	it wasn't.
f There isn't any coffee.		I had.
g My flatmate *will* play his music very loudly.		I hadn't.
h I haven't ironed my shirt.		I didn't.
i I can't go back to bed.		he wouldn't.

2 Join a regret in **A** with a wish in **B**. One line in **B** is used twice.

3 Complete the sentences about Tom's Monday morning blues.

If it _____ Sunday morning, Tom _____ stay in bed till lunchtime.

If his alarm _____ gone off, he _____ have overslept.

If he _____ had too much to drink last night, he _____ feel sick now.

LANGUAGE IN CONTEXT

Past and present wishes

1 Work in pairs. Look at the pictures. Each one illustrates someone's wish. Can you guess what the wish is?

2　T 11.1　Listen to the people expressing wishes. Which wish goes with which picture? Put a letter a–h next to a picture.

3　Complete their wishes.

a　I wish I lived _____ .

b　If only I _____ such a quick-tempered person.

　　If I _____ at George the other day, we _____ friends.

c　I wish _____ faster.

　　I wish _____ longer holidays.

d　If only animals _____ .

e　If only I _____ my car on the double yellow line _____ that ticket.

f　I wish _____ to my grandmother more.

g　I _____ languages.

　　But if I hadn't studied politics, I _____ Andy.

h　I _____ that huge slice of chocolate cake.

4　What are the facts behind each of the wishes and regrets?

　　Example
　　He lives in a cold climate, probably in England.

● Grammar questions

–　Which of these sentences are about the present? Which are about the past?

a　*I wish I **lived** in a warmer climate.*

b　*I wish I **had taken** that job in New York.*

c　*If I **lived** in a warmer climate I **wouldn't get** so many colds.*

d　*If **I'd taken** that job in New York, **I'd have met** the President.*

e　*I'd rather he**'d given** me a gold watch.*

–　All of the sentences express unreality. Which tense is used to express unreality about the present? Which tense expresses unreality about the past?

–　Decontract the verb forms in the last two sentences.

PRACTICE BANK

1　Reading and roleplay

1　T 11.2　Read and listen to the texts about Leanne and Holly. They are both thirty years old, but their lives are very different. Underline like this:

_____ the sentences which express the reality of their lives.

┄┄┄┄┄┄┄┄┄┄ the sentences which express unreality or hypothesis.

Whose life's perfect anyway?

LEANNE KELLY housewife

'Colin and I got married when we were both sixteen. Of course, now I wish we'd waited and I wish I'd had more time to enjoy myself as a teenager, 'cos by the time we were seventeen we had the twins. Now we've got six children, which wouldn't be so bad if Colin wasn't unemployed and if we lived somewhere bigger. This flat has only two tiny bedrooms and it's on the tenth floor. If only there was a park nearby, where the kids could play. I'd rather we had a house with a garden, though. I try to be optimistic but the future's pretty bleak, really.'

HOLLY HARPER magazine editor

'Of course, I know that I'm very lucky. I have a hugely successful career and a beautiful apartment overlooking Central Park. But now I wish I hadn't had to focus so single-mindedly on my work. I know my marriage wouldn't have been such a disaster if I hadn't. I was devastated when Greg and I split up. My mom keeps saying, 'Holly, you're not getting any younger. It's time you started dating again.' I must admit, when I look out of my window at the kids playing in the park, I kinda wish that I lived out of town and had some kids of my own.'

2 Use these words to form conditional sentences.

a Leanne's life/better/if/Colin/a job.
b If/not/married so early/she/time/enjoy her teenage years.
c If/not/married so early/have six children now.
d If Holly/not work hard in the past/she/not have a successful career now.
e If she/spend less time at work/her marriage/not break up.
f If she/not work in New York/she/live in the country.

3 Imagine you are journalists who are going to interview Leanne or Holly for a magazine article. Work together to think of questions you could ask.

4 Work in pairs. One of you is the journalist, the other is Leanne or Holly. Begin the interview like this:
Hello, Leanne/Holly, it's very good of you to agree to be interviewed. Can I begin by asking you how old you are?

2 Wishes to facts

Read the hypotheses and complete the reality. Add a sentence.

Example
I wish I lived in the countryside but *I don't. I live in the town.*

a I wish I spoke English fluently, but …
b If only I didn't get so nervous before exams, but …
c You should have worked harder for your exams, but …
d I'd rather you didn't borrow my things without asking, but …
e I wish my brother wouldn't keep interrupting me when I'm working, but …
f If you'd told me you loved me, we would never have split up, but …
g If my father hadn't gone to work in Malaysia, he wouldn't have met my mother, and I'd never have been born, but …
h It's time those children were in bed, but …

3 Facts to wishes

1 Read the reality and add some wishes. Express them in as many ways as you can.

Example
We went to Blackpool for our holiday and it rained the whole time.
I wish we hadn't gone to Blackpool. If only we'd gone to Spain! We shouldn't have gone to Blackpool. If we'd gone to Spain the weather would have been hot and sunny. I'd rather we'd gone to Spain.

a We didn't have any pets when I was a child because we lived in a flat.
b I have fine, mousey-brown hair and I'm short-sighted.
c My parents really wanted me to become a doctor, not a teacher.
d They think that my youngest brother's a layabout. He won't even look for a job.
e I come from a huge family. I've got seven brothers and one sister.
f I can't remember my grandmother because she died when I was only three.
g I didn't start learning a foreign language until I was fifteen.
h I didn't get the job I applied for in Barcelona because I can't speak Spanish.

2 What do you wish was different about your family? Your work? Your school? You?

4 *Would* or *had*?

T 11.3 Listen to the sentences. They all contain 'd. Say if 'd = *would* or *had*.

Examples
I wish he'd listen. = *would*
If he'd listened, I'd have understood. = *had* and *would*

LANGUAGE REVIEW

Hypothesis

Tenses can be used to express both fact and non-fact (hypothesis). Tenses which express fact refer to *real* time.

*I **have** a boring job. I **don't earn** much money.* (Present fact)
*I **didn't work** hard. I **failed** all my exams.* (Past fact)

Tenses that express non-fact do *not* refer to real time. The verb moves *one tense back* to show unreality.

*I wish I **had** a good job. If only I **earned** more money.*
*I wish I'd (= had) **worked** harder. If only I **hadn't failed** all my exams.* (Non-facts)

Hypothesizing about the present

The Past Simple is used in the second conditional, and with *wish*, *if only*, *would rather* and *it's time* to express unreal present and future.

*If I **had** enough money,*
  *I'd **buy** a new car.* (I don't have enough money.)
*I wish I **were** (or **was**) rich.* (I'm not rich.)
*If only I **had** a new car.* (I have an old one.)
*I wish I **could** come.* (I can't come.)
*I wish you **would** help*
  with the housework. (You won't/don't help.)
*I'd rather you **lived** nearer.* (You live miles away.)
*It's time you **knew** the truth.* (You don't know it.)

Hypothesizing about the past

The Past Perfect is used in the third conditional, and with *wish*, *if only*, and *would rather* to express unreal or imaginary past.

*If he'd **been** more careful, he **wouldn't have fallen**.*
(He wasn't careful. He fell.)
*I wish I'd **met** the President.*
(I didn't meet/I haven't met the President.)

Should + the perfect infinitive is used to refer to a past action that didn't happen. The action would have been a good idea. It is advice that is too late!
*You **should have taken** the medicine.*
(You didn't take it.)

📖 **Grammar reference: page 141.**

● LISTENING AND READING

Things we never said

Listening

1 Friends often lose touch with each other. Do you have any friends you have lost touch with? What memories do you have of these friends? Would you like to meet them again?

2 **T 11.4** You are going to listen to a short radio play. It is about two friends, Peter and Amanda, who meet again after some years. They are in their home town. Listen and answer the questions.

a Did they arrange to meet? How do you know?
b Why have they returned to their home town?
c Where do they live now?
d Have they kept in touch over the years? How do you know?
e What ambitions did they have when they were younger? Did these ambitions become reality?

3 The play is based on a short story called *Things we never said*. What can you predict about the full story? Consider these questions in pairs.

– How old do you think Peter and Amanda were when they first knew each other?
– What was their relationship?
– Why did they lose touch? Did they miss each other?
– What are their families like?
– Are they now married?
– Are they happy with their present lives?
– Do they have any regrets?
– Will they meet again soon?

Read the complete story. Compare your ideas with what you learn in the story.
Do you feel sorry for Peter and Amanda, or angry with them? Why? What is tragic about them?

Things we never said
by Fiona Goble

He saw her from behind and recognized her immediately. He walked faster until he was just ahead of her, then turned round, wondering whether to smile. It didn't seem like fifteen years. She didn't see him at first. She was looking in
5 a shop window. He touched the sleeve of her jacket.

'Hello, Amanda,' he said gently. He knew he hadn't made a mistake. Not this time. For years he kept thinking he'd seen her – at bus stops, in pubs, at parties.

'Peter!' As she said his name, her heart quickened. She
10 remembered their first summer together. They'd lain together by the river at Cliveden. They were both 18 and he'd rested his head on her stomach, twisting grass in his fingers, and told her that he couldn't live without her.

'I'm surprised you recognize me,' he said, burying his
15 hands in the pockets of his coat.

'Really?' She smiled. In fact she'd been thinking about him a lot recently. 'You haven't moved back here, have you?' Surely not, she thought. She knew he loathed the place. Even at 18, he couldn't wait to leave and travel
20 the world.

'Good heavens no,' he said. 'I'm still in London.'

She looked at him. He looked the same. He hadn't begun to go bald like so many of the men she knew, but his shoulders were broader and his face slightly rounder.

25 'I came back for the funeral,' he continued. 'My father's. A heart attack. It happened very suddenly.'

'I'm sorry,' she said, though she wasn't really. She remembered him telling her about how his father used to beat him regularly until he was 16 and grew too tall.

30 'Thank you,' he said to her, though he felt nothing for his dead father, just relief for his mother. She'd be happier without him. She'd been trying to pluck up courage to leave him for years.

'And I take it that you're not living back here either?'

35 'I'm in London, too,' she said. She pushed her hair behind her ears in a gesture that he hadn't forgotten.

'Just back for my sister's wedding tomorrow.'

'That's nice,' he said, though his only memory of Amanda's sister was as a rather plump, boring 12-year-old.

40 'Yes,' she agreed, feeling that her baby sister's wedding only served to spotlight her own series of failed relationships.

'And your parents?' he asked. 'They're well?'

'Fine.' She remembered how he'd always envied
45 her middle-class parents, who ate foreign food and took exotic holidays.

'Are you rushing off somewhere?' he asked.

'No, I'm just killing time, really.'

'Then I suggest we kill it together. Let's grab a coffee.'

50 They walked towards Gaby's, a small café just off the high street. They had spent hours there when they had first met, laughing and holding hands under the table, and discussing their plans for the future over cups of coffee. They sat opposite each other. He ordered the coffee.

55 'And so, Peter, did you become a foreign correspondent?' she asked, remembering the places they dreamed of visiting together – India, Morocco, and Australia.

'Not exactly,' he said. 'I'm a lawyer, believe it or not.' She
60 looked at his clothes, and she could believe it. They were a far cry from the second-hand shirts and jeans he'd worn as a student.

'You enjoy it?' she asked.

'Yes,' he lied. 'And you? Are you a world famous artist?'
65 He'd always loved her pictures. He remembered the portrait of herself which she'd painted for him for his twentieth birthday. He still had it.

'Well, … no.' She tried to laugh. She wondered if he still had her self-portrait. She'd stopped painting years ago. He
70 looked at her hair, cascading in dark unruly waves over her shoulders. He could see a few white hairs now, but she was still very beautiful.

'So,' he said. 'What are you up to?'

'Nothing much,' she said. 'I've tried a few things.' She
75 didn't want to tell him about the succession of temporary jobs that she'd hoped might lead to something more permanent but never had.

'So you're not painting at all?'

'Only doors and walls,' she joked, and he laughed
80 politely. She remembered the evenings they'd spent in the small bedsit that they rented together in their last term at college. He'd sit for hours just watching her paint. She filled sketch book after sketch book.

'So where are you in London?' she asked.

85 'North,' he said. It was a three-bedroom flat in Hampstead. Nice in an empty kind of way. He thought

about all the evenings he wished he had someone to come home to.

'And you?' he asked, after a pause.

90 'South. It's okay, I rent a room.' She thought of the small room with the damp walls which she rented in an unfashionable part of Clapham. 'But I'm thinking of buying somewhere. It's one of the reasons I came home. I want to sort things out a bit,' she sighed, thinking about the letters

95 from him that she'd found in her old bedroom. She'd been reading them only yesterday.

'Oh, Peter, I don't know why I left that day,' she said at last. He looked up at her.

'It's all right,' he said, remembering the evening she

100 hadn't come back to the bedsit.

'We were young. Young people do things like that all the time,' he added, knowing that this wasn't true, knowing that he hadn't deserved such treatment. He thought of all the letters he'd sent to her parents' home. He'd written

105 every day at first, begging her to return or at least to ring him. He'd known even then that he would never meet anyone like her again.

'I suppose you're right.' She swallowed hard, trying to hide her disappointment and hurt that he seemed to have

110 no regrets.

'Well, I ought to be going,' she said.

'Already? I thought you had time to kill.'

'I did,' she said, blinking to hold back the tears. 'But I ought to get back now to help my mother with

115 the wedding.'

'I understand,' he said, though he didn't. Surely her parents would understand?

'Shall I give you my phone number. Perhaps we could meet up?'

120 'Perhaps,' she said.

He wrote his telephone number on the back of the bill and she tucked it into the zipped compartment of her handbag.

'Thanks. Goodbye, Peter.'

125 'Goodbye, Amanda.'

Years later, every so often, she still checked that compartment to make sure his number was there.

Comprehension check

1 Are the following statements true (✔) or false (✘)? Correct the false ones.

a Peter and Amanda used to be in love.

b They are now both 33 years old.

c They both still look exactly the same.

d His mother is distraught over his father's death.

e Amanda's sister is twelve years old.

f Amanda hasn't had another boyfriend since Peter.

g Only Peter has had the career that he planned.

h They both live alone now.

i Peter was broken-hearted when Amanda left him.

j Amanda is on the verge of tears because Peter seems so cold and dispassionate.

k He still loves her, but she doesn't love him any more.

2 Close your books. Listen again to the play. Your teacher will stop the tape after every few lines. How much of the full story can you recall?

Roleplay

1 Divide into two groups.

Group A Make a list of Peter's problems. What are his regrets?

Group B Make a list of Amanda's problems. What are her regrets?

2 Work with a partner. One of you is Peter and the other is Amanda. You meet again. This time you tell each other the truth about your lives. Begin like this:

Do you want to know the truth? Well, I wish we hadn't split up, I hate my job. I still think about you a lot. And what about you? How do you really feel? Are you happy?

Language work

1 The following parts of the body appear in the text. In what connection are they mentioned?

head	heart (x2)	stomach
shoulders (x2)	face	hands (x2)
hair (x2)	hairs	fingers	ears

2 What part of speech are these words? Which parts of the body are they connected with?

bald	blink	waves	swallow	beat
tears	plump			

●VOCABULARY

Idioms

Use your dictionary to check new words and expressions.

A

1 Read the sentences and answer the questions.

I had time to kill	
I was at a loose end	so I went to a café and had a coffee.
I was early and needed to pass the time	
I was bored and had nothing else to do	

a Which of the sentences contain idioms? <u>Underline</u> them.
b Which sentences do not contain idiomatic expressions?
c Which pairs of sentences have the same meaning?
d Under which word did you find the idiom in your dictionary?

2 Work in pairs. Do the same with these groups of sentences.

a This house | is a far cry from | where we used to live.
      | isn't nearly as nice as |
      | is very different from |
      | isn't a patch on |

b A lot of water has flowed under the bridge | since we last met.
   I've become much more successful |
   So much has happened |
   I've gone up in the world |

c After just six months' trading, my uncle's business | went down the drain.
   | became very successful.
   | went bankrupt.
   | hit the jackpot.

d His name's on the tip of my tongue, | but I have such a terrible memory.
   His name rings a bell, |
   I'll remember his name in a minute, |
   His name sounds familiar, |

3 Match a cartoon in **A** with one of these idioms.

> get cold feet   go through the roof   bury your head in the sand
> have butterflies in your stomach   break someone's heart   break the ice
> fall head over heels in love   be over the moon

4 The idioms are illustrated literally in **A** and idiomatically in **B**. Try to work out the meanings of the idioms.

5 Complete the sentences with the correct idiom from Exercise 3.
   You will sometimes need to make changes to fit the context.

a When I won a trip for two to Venice I …
b She doesn't want to hear about her husband and his secretary, she just …
c The party was very tense until Ian told some of his funny stories. This …
d They have eyes for nobody else. When they met, they …
e I was so nervous when I went for the interview for that job. I …
f My father will be furious when he hears I've crashed his car. He …
g I didn't go on that blind date, because at the last minute I …
h When I discovered he'd been unfaithful, it …

B

● LISTENING AND WRITING

Family secrets

You are going to hear two unusual family stories.

Pre-listening task

1 Do you come from a big or small family? How many brothers, sisters, aunts, uncles, cousins do you have?

2 Study this family tree. Discuss these questions with a partner.

a What is the relationship between:
Deborah and Ralph?
Christine and Ruth?
Christine and Yuri?
Christine and Clive and Isuzu?

b In the story Deborah learns of a family secret. What do you think it might be?

c Why do you think Ralph is known as the 'black sheep' of the family?

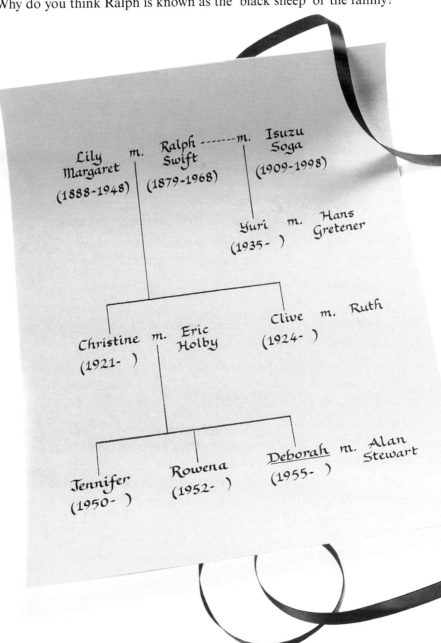

Listening and writing

Part 1

My Japanese aunt

T 11.5 Listen to Deborah talking about her family. As you listen, look at the family tree and circle the people she talks about. Most of them are not mentioned by name. Who are they in relation to Deborah?

Comprehension check

1 Answer the questions.

a Why does Deborah think that her grandfather is not really a 'black sheep'?
b Three jobs are mentioned. What are they? Whose are they?
c Whose is the baby mentioned? What's the name of the baby?
d Where and how did Deborah and her sisters learn the family secret?
e What is Christine's attitude to her father's behaviour?
f What does she wish that Ruth hadn't done?
g Why did Deborah find her visit to Japan so amazing?
h How old was she when she went there?
i How old were Isuzu and Yuri when Deborah met them?

2 This is a dramatic reconstruction of the conversation at the dinner table when the family secret came out.

a Read the scene and complete Christine's telling of the story.

> **Ruth** (wiping her mouth on a napkin) *Christine, I've been meaning to ask you. Did you ever hear again from Yuri and her mother?*
>
> **Christine** (coughs and splutters over her meal. Then replies icily.) *I'd rather we didn't talk about that.*
>
> **Deborah, Rowena, and Jennifer** (very puzzled and interested) *Who's Yuri?*
>
> **Ruth** (sounding very surprised) *Don't you know? Surely, Christine, you've told them about their Aunt Yuri?*
>
> **Deborah** (amazed) *Aunt? But you're our only aunt! We've never heard of an Aunt Yuri. Who is she, Mother?* (she turns accusingly to her mother) *You've got to tell us.*
>
> **Christine** (sighs deeply then laughs nervously) *Oh, well, I suppose you had to find out some time. It all happened many years ago. But if you really want to know* (she takes a deep breath) *I'll tell you.* (pause) *You remember that your grandfather was a silk dealer, and for many years he and your grandmother lived in Japan. Well, what happened was this ...*

b Finish the scene with the comments and reactions of the other characters. Include stage directions as in the piece above.
c Act out the scene in groups.

Part 2

My Canadian aunt

Listen to a lady called Connie talking about the birth of her great aunt.

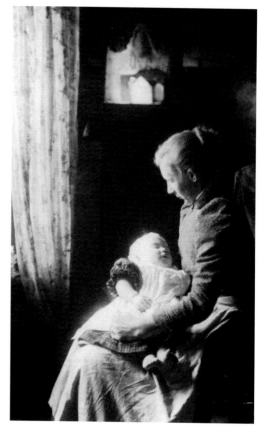

Comprehension check

Answer the questions.

– Where and when was her great aunt born?
– Who was present at the birth?
– What was the problem? Who solved the problem and how?
– What would have happened if the oven had not been on?

Writing a play

Write a short play based on Connie's story with full stage directions.

Discussion

Do you know of any interesting stories about your family? Tell the rest of the class about them, but only if you want to!

PostScript

Moans and groans

1 Read the complaints in **A**. Match them with a response in **B**. Which of the items below do they refer to? Write a number in the box and an item on the line.

> a painting   a sweater   a tin opener   shoes   homework
> a meal   a TV programme   a washing machine   an exam

a ☐ _____   b ☐ _____   c ☐ _____

d ☐ _____   e ☐ _____   f ☐ _____

g ☐ _____   h ☐ _____   i ☐ _____

A	B
a So why didn't you hand it in on time? I'm not going to mark it now.	
b It's always the same. I hummed and hawed about getting it, then when I went back it had been sold and it was one of his best works.	1 Here, give it to me! Let me try.
c Ouch! I've had it with this thing. It just doesn't work.	2 Sorry. I forgot. I was in a hurry.
d It's not fair. I'd been looking forward to watching it all day and then the phone goes and rings!	3 I'm awfully sorry, sir. I'm afraid there's nothing I can do about it.
e How many times do I have to tell you? Take them off *before* you come into the house!	4 You're not kidding! Massive prices and lousy food!
f This has gone beyond a joke. You promised you'd deliver it by Tuesday at the latest. Now you're saying next month!	5 But, I'm really sorry. I just didn't have the chance to finish it at the weekend.
g I could kick myself. As soon as I'd handed in the paper, I remembered what the answer was.	6 But do you think you've still passed?
h Of course, they didn't have it in red. Apparently, it only comes in navy blue.	7 You should have asked if you could put a deposit on it.
i It's the last time I'll eat here.	8 But wouldn't that go well with your white jeans?
	9 And who was it? Anyone interesting?

2 **T 11.6** Listen and check your answers.

3 What are some of the events in a typical day in your life? For each event think of something to moan about.

4 What's happened recently? Do you have any moans and groans about the things that have happened?

12 Icons

Noun phrases
Adding emphasis
Linking and commenting

Test your grammar

Match the words in the box with a picture. Then use the words to make one sentence about each picture.

Example

a *He's a grey-haired businessman with a rose in his button hole.*

> with a thatched roof   which expires in February 2020
> wearing a uniform   country   pair of
> roses growing round the front door   dirty
> ~~grey-haired~~   ~~business~~   ~~in his button hole~~
> giving someone a parking ticket   traffic   football
> ~~with a rose~~   sitting on a wall   driving
> licking an ice-cream   stuffed in a bag

LANGUAGE IN CONTEXT

Noun phrases and adding emphasis

1 Read text **A**. Your teacher will give you some questions.

> ### Text A
>
> Michelangelo (1475–1564) was one of the most inspired creators in the history of art. He had a tremendous influence on all his contemporaries, as a sculptor, an architect, a painter, and a poet.
>
> He was born near Arezzo, but he considered Florence to be his home town. He loved the city's art, architecture, and culture above all.
>
> He concentrated on sculpture initially. He began to carve a figure of David from a huge block of marble in 1501. He finished it in 1504, when he was 29. He shows David with a sling on his shoulder, looking into the distance.
>
> Pope Julius II asked Michelangelo to paint the ceiling of the Sistine Chapel later. Michelangelo worked on this task every day for four years from 1508 till 1512, lying on his back at the top of high scaffolding, his neck stiff, with paint trickling onto his face.
>
> Many buildings were designed by him. His work at St Peter's Basilica represented his greatest achievement as an architect. His dome became the model for domes all over the Western world. Its revolutionary design is difficult to appreciate nowadays.
>
> Michelangelo belongs to that small group of artists such as Shakespeare and Beethoven, who have been able to express the deepest experiences of humanity through their work.

2 Read text **B**. Compare the two texts. The information is the same, but there are differences. Which one sounds better?

*M*ichelangelo (1475–1564) was one of the most inspired creators in the history of art. As a sculptor, an architect, a painter, and a poet, he had a tremendous influence on all his contemporaries.

He was born near Arezzo, but it was Florence that he considered to be his home town. What he loved above all was the city's art, architecture, and culture.

Initially, he concentrated on sculpture. In 1501 he began to carve a figure of David from a huge block of marble. This was finished in 1504, when he was 29. David is shown with a sling on his shoulder, looking into the distance.

Later, Michelangelo was asked by Pope Julius II to paint the ceiling of the Sistine Chapel. Every day for four years, from 1508 till 1512, he worked on this task, lying on his back at the top of high scaffolding, his neck stiff, with paint trickling onto his face.

He designed many buildings, but it was his work at St Peter's Basilica that represented his greatest achievement as an architect. His dome became the model for domes all over the Western world. What is difficult to appreciate nowadays is its revolutionary design.

There is a small group of artists such as Shakespeare and Beethoven, who, through their work, have been able to express the deepest experiences of humanity. Michelangelo belongs to this group.

3 Close your book. Your teacher will give you a copy of Text **B** with gaps. Fill the gaps with one of the words in the box.

a	an	the	(nothing = zero article)	his	all
this	its	every	their		

● Grammar questions

– How does word order change the emphasis in a sentence?

– Find sentences in Text **B** beginning *It was …* and *What …* that express emphasis. How are they different from those in Text **A**?

– Find examples of passive sentences with and without *by*. Where is the focus of attention in these sentences?

PRACTICE BANK

1 Adding emphasis

Rephrase the sentences to make them more emphatic.

Example
I like Tony's honesty.

What The thing	I like about Tony is	his honesty. the way the fact that	he always tells the truth.

a My daughter is very untidy. This annoys me.
b Tom's very generous. I like this.
c I can't stand my son's moodiness.
d I admire the Italians' love of life.
e The Germans' sense of duty makes them work hard.
f The reliability of Mercedes Benz cars makes them so popular.
g I can never resist chocolate desserts in a restaurant.

2 Emphasis and sentence stress

1 When we speak, we can stress the important part of a sentence with our voice.

T 12.1 Listen to the examples.

Examples
'Who gave you that new car?' '**Susan** gave it to me.'
'Did she sell it to you?' 'No, she **gave** it to me.'
'Did she give it to Peter?' 'No, she gave it to **me**.'
'Is it second-hand?' 'No, it's **new**.'
'Did she give you a new stereo?' 'No, she gave me a new **car**.'

T 12.2 Listen to the questions about these sentences. Then say the sentences with the correct stress. Change the sentences as necessary.

a Ann gave David a blue shirt for his birthday.
b James flew to Paris for a month to learn French.
c We go to Scotland every autumn because we like walking.
d My eldest son is studying law at Bristol university.

2 In pairs, ask similar questions about these sentences. Answer with the appropriate stress.

a Dave phoned me yesterday and invited me to his wedding.

b My wife and I are going to travel round Europe for three months by train.

c Mark lost a wallet with £50 in it while he was jogging in the park.

d I'm meeting Jane at half past seven outside the cinema.

3 Where is the stress in the second line of these dialogues?

a 'Why weren't you at school yesterday?'
'I *was* at school.'

b 'Come on, Dave. It's time to get up.'
'I *am* getting up.'

c 'It's a shame you don't like parties.'
'But I *do* like parties!'

d 'I wish you'd tidy your room.'
'I *have* tidied it.'

e 'What a shame you didn't see Tom.'
'I *did* see Tom.'

T12.3 Listen and check your answers. Note that if there is no auxiliary verb, we add *do/does/did*.

4 Your teacher will read out some sentences. Correct him/her.

Example
I never give you any homework.
*You **do** give us homework. Lots!*

3 Active or passive?

Complete the sentences. Use the verb in the active or the passive, depending where the focus of attention is.

a Yesterday, the murder trial of James Kent came to an end. _____ (sentence) to ten years' imprisonment.

b Judge Robert Henderson decided to make an example of Steve Phillips, who had been arrested for burglary for the thirtieth time. _____ (sentence) to four years' imprisonment.

c Flight attendants are always very busy. _____ (show) passengers how to put on a lifejacket, and _____ (serve) food and drinks.

d Every attempt is made so that airline passengers feel safe and comfortable. _____ (show) how to put on a lifejacket, and _____ (serve) food and drinks.

e Good luck with your new job in Italy. I'm sure _____ (tell) what you have to do when you arrive.

f Your new boss is Donatella Morno. _____ (tell) what you have to do.

4 Articles and determiners

1 Correct the mistakes in the sentences.

a I had the lunch with a colleague.
b Do you do business in States?
c I came here in one taxi.
d The unemployment is a world problem these days.
e I'm reading a book about life of Beethoven at the moment.
f My sister broke the leg skiing.
g Computer has changed our lives completely.
h I have only an ambition in life, and that is to be rich.
i She works as interpreter for United Nations.
j 'Where's your mother?' 'In a kitchen.'
k 'Would you like a drink?' 'Yes, I'd love it.'
l Tell me a truth. Do you love me or not?
m Last night we went to the restaurant. Food was good, but a service was terrible.

2 Have a class discussion. How are men and women different?

Men are more logical.
Women are more instinctive.
Men like talking about things.
Women like talking about people.

3 Match a line in **A** with a line in **B**.

A		B
Would you like		eggs?
Do all birds lay		the egg?
Where did I put		an egg?
I have two cars. Borrow		each one.
I said goodbye to		everyone.
I have five nieces, I gave a present to		either one.

A	B	
Love	I have for you is forever.	
A love	is everything.	
The love	of animals is vital for a vet.	
Both	my friends like dancing.	
All	student in my class is friendly.	
Every	my parents are Scottish.	

5 Speaking

Each student should prepare a short talk on one of the following topics.

• A person you admire
• A hero or icon
• A pet hate
Try to include some of the ways of expressing emphasis.

LANGUAGE REVIEW

Noun phrases

1 Information can be added before and after a noun.

*a **grey-haired** businessman **with a rose in his button hole***
*a driving licence **which expires in 2020***

2 Articles and determiners refer to nouns.

*Cordoba is **a** city in the south of Spain.*
*My brother works in **the** City of London.*
( ) Cities are ( ) exciting places. (= zero article)

each/every/either boy (singular noun)
both/all girls (plural noun)

this/that man
these/those women

Adding emphasis

There are many ways of adding emphasis to a text, such as the passive, word order, using certain emphatic structures, and auxiliaries.

***In 1504** Michelangelo finished the statue of David.*
***The statue of David was finished** in 1504.*

What
The thing that | *annoys me is people who are always late.*

*It's people like you **who** are ruining the country.*

*I **did** tidy my room! Honest!*

📖 **Grammar reference: page 142.**

● READING AND SPEAKING

It blows your mind!

Pre-reading task

1 Look at the photos. What do you know about the first atomic bomb test?

2 Work in pairs. Discuss whether this information is true or false.

a The atomic bomb was first tested just before the Second World War.
b The atomic bomb was developed by a team of American scientists.
c The first atomic explosion took place on an island in the Pacific.
d US marines were deliberately exposed to radiation to monitor its effects.
e It was hoped that the atomic bomb would end all wars.
f Albert Einstein was involved in the creation of the bomb.
g Atomic bombs were used against Japan just three weeks after the first test bomb.
h Everyone agreed that it was right to use the weapons against Japan.
i At the time German scientists were close to developing the atomic bomb.

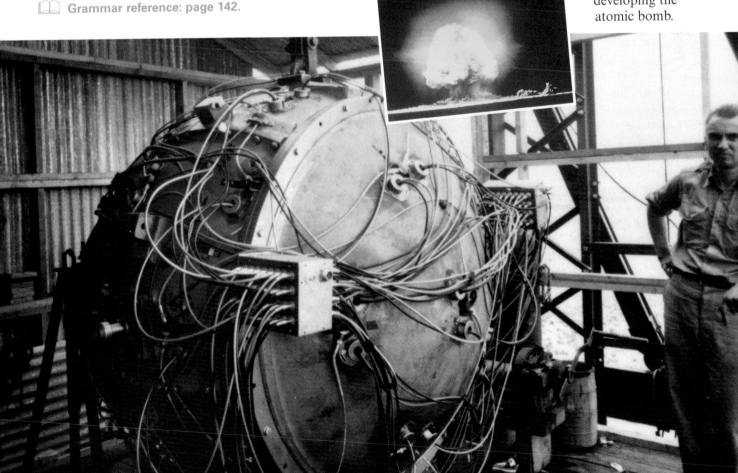

Read the article about the first atomic explosion. Which of the questions on page 121 can you now answer?

'I am become Death, the destroyer of worlds'

The first explosion of the atom bomb, on July 16, 1945, was summed up by Robert Oppenheimer with these words from a Hindu poem.

Peter Millar reports on the race led by Oppenheimer, the brilliant physicist, at Los Alamos, New Mexico, to create the weapon that would end the Second World War.

In the foothills of the New Mexican mountains, on a dusty desert plain known as the Jornada del Muerto – Dead Man's Journey – camped the greatest collection of scientific brains on earth. They were men who would redefine the 20th century: Robert Oppenheimer (American), Enrico Fermi (Italian), George Kistiakowski (Ukrainian), Otto Frisch (Austrian), General Leslie Groves (American), Edward Teller (Hungarian), and Klaus Fuchs (born in Germany, but a naturalized Briton).

Better than any men in the world, they should have known what to expect in those still minutes before dawn in the desert. But none of them knew for sure what would happen. The explosion at 05.29 on the morning of July 16, 1945, stunned its creators and changed the world: the atomic bomb worked.

There were several eye-witness accounts of that first atomic explosion. 'It blasted; it pounced; it bored its way right through you. It was a vision which was seen with more than the eye. It seemed to last forever. You longed for it to stop. Altogether it lasted about two seconds. Finally it was over.' Another observer wrote: 'It was like a ball of fire, too bright to look at directly. The whole surface of the ball was covered with a purple luminosity.' His report ends: 'I am sure that all who witnessed this test went away with a profound feeling that they had seen one of the great events in history.'

Los Alamos today supports a community of just over 18,000 people. On first impressions it is like many other small towns in western America: full of low two-storey buildings, dusty, with rather dingy shopping malls, a couple of banks, filling stations, Mexican and Chinese fast-food joints, a motel, and a McDonald's. But there are plenty of indications that this is no ordinary town. Big blue signs along State Highway 84 advise travellers that the road and land on either side belong to the US government. A notice declares that it is 'forbidden to remove dirt'. At one point a high watchtower stands sentry behind a twenty-foot barbed-wire fence.

Before 1942, however, Los Alamos had no history because it didn't exist. It was created for one purpose only, to house the technicians who would make the bomb before anyone else did. All mail was censored, and everyone was sworn to secrecy. The US government did not even trust its own protégés. Oppenheimer, who had mixed with left-wing groups in his youth, was tailed by FBI men. Einstein, who had written to President Roosevelt in 1939 urging him to develop the atomic bomb, was ruled out because of his outspoken pacifism and Zionism. Yet the real villain went undetected. Klaus Fuchs was revealed in 1950 as Stalin's spy.

What is interesting is that the scientists were much more interested in sharing the bomb with the Russians than the politicians were. Some physicists dreamed of the bomb as an end to all wars, a possible means of establishing global government. As it progressed from a theoretical possiblity to an experimental reality, concern grew among some of those involved about how it would be used. By early 1945, Germany, the original target, no longer needed an atomic explosion to force its surrender. Attention switched to Japan.

In 1943 Harold Argo was a graduate from Washington University when he was summoned to New Mexico. Now over 80, he describes his time at Los Alamos as 'the most exciting two years of my life'. He dismisses those whose consciences troubled them. 'I don't understand all those sceptics who had second thoughts. I had two brothers out there in the Pacific. If Harry Truman hadn't dropped the bomb, the war could have gone on forever.'

Carson Mark is more reflective. 'At the time, we thought it would put an end to organized war, because no one can put up with destruction on that scale. But

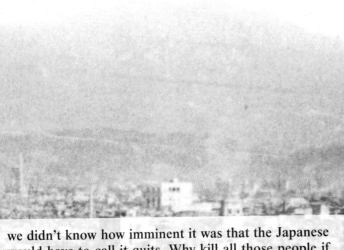

we didn't know how imminent it was that the Japanese would have to call it quits. Why kill all those people if you don't need to?'

In May 1945 nobody was sure just how devastating the bomb would be. There was general agreement that the simpler type of bomb would work, but the more complicated plutonium implosion device would need testing. Oppenheimer named the test Trinity, partly because of the Christian concept of God the Father, the Son, and the Holy Spirit, but mainly because of the Hindu three-in-one godhead of Vishnu, Brahma, and Siva, the power of life, the creator, and destroyer.

The site selected was 33 miles from the nearest town. The VIP observation site was located 20 miles away. The scientists had a bet with each other to guess how many tonnes' equivalent of TNT their bomb would produce. So imprecise was their knowledge that Oppenheimer conservatively suggested 300. Teller, wiser, speculated an incredible 45,000. Radiochemical analysis revealed the blast had equalled 18,600 tonnes of TNT, four times what most of those involved on the project had guessed.

Even as they were celebrating at Los Alamos, hours after the explosion, the warship *Indianapolis* sailed out of San Francisco harbour, carrying the atomic bomb nicknamed *Little Boy* on its fateful voyage to the island of Tinian in the Pacific. After unloading its deadly cargo, the ship sailed on towards the Philippines. On July 29 it was sunk by a Japanese submarine; of the 850 who survived the sinking, more than 500 were eaten alive by sharks.

On Tinian, group commander Paul Tibbets had his B-29 bomber repainted, and he gave it his mother's name, Enola Gay. In Hiroshima and Nagasaki, the citizens slept.

Just three weeks after the test, the bomb was used for real. As the historian Richard Rhodes wrote in his book *The Making of the Atomic Bomb*, 'Once Trinity proved that the atomic bomb worked, men discovered reasons to use it.'

Comprehension check

1 Explain the title of the article.

2 Answer the questions.

a Did the scientists know exactly what would happen when the first bomb exploded?
  Did they expect it to be bigger or smaller?
b How did they feel when it went off?
c How did the eye-witnesses describe it?
d What are the indications that Los Alamos is no ordinary town?
e Why isn't the town on any map before 1942?
f Why did the scientists want to share their knowledge with the Russians?
  Why do you think the politicians didn't agree with them?
g In what way do Harold Argo and Carson Mark have different opinions?
h What do you know about the warship *Indianapolis*?
i When and where was the first atomic bomb used in warfare?

3 Who are these people? What does the text say about them?

a the greatest collection of scientific brains (l. 7–8)
b none of them (l. 17)
c its creators (l. 19)
d a community (l. 33)
e travellers (l. 41)
f the technicians (l. 48)
g its own protégés (l. 51)
h the real villain (l. 56)
i the original target (l. 67)
j all those sceptics (l. 74)
k God (l. 89)
l VIP (l. 94)
m *Little Boy* (l. 106)
n Enola Gay (l. 114)

Language work

1 What is the subject of these sentences from the text?

a In the foothills of the New Mexican mountains … camped the greatest collection of scientific brains on earth. (l. 5–8)
b So imprecise was their knowledge that Oppenheimer conservatively suggested 300. (l. 97–8)
  What is the effect of changing the normal word order?

2 Comment on the use of the passive in these sentences. Where is the focus of attention?

a All mail was censored, and everyone was sworn to secrecy. (l. 49–50)
b Oppenheimer … was tailed by FBI men. (l. 52–3)
c Klaus Fuchs was revealed in 1950 as Stalin's spy. (l. 57–8)
d … it was sunk by a Japanese submarine … (l. 109)
e … more than 500 were eaten alive by sharks. (l. 110–1)

What do you think?

1 How did the atomic bomb alter the course of history in the twentieth century?
2 Do you agree with the historian Richard Rhodes?

● VOCABULARY

Homophones

1 Homophones are words with the same pronunciation but different spelling and different meaning.

/wɔ:/ *war* and *wore*
/haɪə/ *higher* and *hire*

Think of two spellings for these words in phonemic script. One of the two words is in lines 5 to 24 of the text about the atomic bomb.

a /nju:/ _____

b /pleɪn/ _____ _____

c /ʃɔ:/ _____ _____

d /wʊd/ _____ _____

e /si:n/ _____ _____

f /θru:/ _____ _____

2 Think of two spellings for these words in phonemic script.

a /pi:s/ _____ _____

b /kɔ:t/ _____ _____

c /weɪ/ _____ _____

d /'weðə/ _____ _____

e /meɪl/ _____ _____

f /saɪt/ _____ _____

Homonyms

1 Homonyms are words with the same spelling and pronunciation but different meanings.

a dusty desert **plain**   the **plain** truth
a **plain** white blouse   **plain** food

Fill the pairs of gaps with the same word. Sometimes the word changes its form.
The words occur from the title to line 40 of the text about the atomic bomb.

a The film _____ an hour. It was great.

I came _____ in the race.

b There were several different _____ of the story in the newspapers.

My wife and I have a joint _____ at our bank.

c I was left a small _____ of money by my aunt.

Can I _____ up the meeting before we end?

d It is illegal to discriminate against people on grounds of sex, _____ , or religion.

I'm exhausted. I've been _____ around all day – working, shopping, and cooking.

e The queue was so _____ that I didn't wait.

Rain, rain, rain! I'm fed up with it. I'm _____ for some sunshine.

f _____ your name here, please.

What does that _____ on the wall mean?

g Keep _____ . Don't move.

She didn't do any revision, but she _____ passed the exam.

2 Think of two meanings for these words. Write sentences that illustrate the different meanings.

match	draw	cross	fine	fair	fit	suit
miss	mind	mark	sentence	point		

Children's jokes

T 12.4 A lot of jokes are made with homophones and homonyms because there is a play on words. Listen to these children's jokes.

● LISTENING

Great events of the twentieth century

Pre-listening task

1 Look at the photos. What famous events of the twentieth century do they illustrate? Can you put a date to each photo?

2 Work in groups of four.
Think of the greatest event of the twentieth century for each of these categories.

Politics (P)	War (W)
Medicine (M)	Social changes (SC)
Transport (Tr)	Art and culture (AC)
Technology (Tech)	Sport (S)

3 Discuss your conclusions as a class.

Listening

T 12.5 You will hear people expressing opinions on the great events of the twentieth century. What is the event? What category of event is it? Put a letter from Exercise 2 opposite. Often you will need to write more than one letter.

Speaker	Event	Category
Pam		
David		
Alexa		
Penny		
Pam		
David		
Hilary		
Barry		

Comprehension check

1 Did any of them mention the same event as you?

2 Answer the questions.

a What is the image that Pam has in her mind?
How did the crowds feel?
How did *she* feel?

b What, for David, is the most surprising aspect of the collapse of communism?
Does he express a personal opinion on whether capitalism is preferable to communism?

c What does Alexa say is strange about conversations on the Internet?
In what way are they different from face-to-face conversations?

d How has Penny benefited from feminism?

e What is Pam's anecdote about penicillin?

f What, according to David, is the big problem for the twenty-first century?

g Why does Hilary say that the First World War was the main event of the century?
What does she say about life in the 1900s and life in the 1920s?

h What is silly about Barry's suggestion, and what is not?
What, according to Barry, did young people use to do?
What was different after Elvis?
Why was society ripe for a change?

Focusing attention

1 Read the texts about Elvis Presley. Choose which version sounds better, a or b.
  Think about word order, and where the focus of attention is.

1 ☐   2 ☐   3 ☐   4 ☐   5 ☐   6 ☐   7 ☐
8 ☐   9 ☐   10 ☐

1 (a) **Elvis Presley** (1935–1977) was a rock and roll singer whose enormous success changed popular culture throughout the world.	(b) Popular culture throughout the world was changed by the enormous success of **Elvis Presley** (1935–1977), a rock and roll singer.
2 (a) His parents raised Presley in Memphis, where he sang at church services.	(b) Presley was raised in Memphis, where he sang at church services.
3 (a) As a teenager, he taught himself to play the guitar.	(b) He taught himself to play the guitar as a teenager.
4 (a) Sam Phillips was a rhythm and blues producer, and Presley recorded songs for him in July 1954.	(b) In July 1954 Presley recorded songs for Sam Phillips, a rhythm and blues producer.
5 (a) What earned him the nickname 'Elvis the Pelvis' was his charismatic style on stage.	(b) His charismatic style on stage earned him the nickname 'Elvis the Pelvis'.
6 (a) About this time Presley met Colonel Tom Parker, a promoter who managed the rest of his career.	(b) The rest of Presley's career was managed by a promoter, Colonel Tom Parker, who Presley met about this time.
7 (a) In 1956 Presley released *Heartbreak Hotel*, the first of 45 records that sold more than a million copies each.	(b) It was 45 records that Presley released that sold more than a million copies each, and the first of these was *Heartbreak Hotel* in 1956.
8 (a) Viewers saw him only from the waist up when he frequently appeared on television because people considered his dancing was too sexually suggestive.	(b) He frequently appeared on television, but because his dancing was considered too sexually suggestive, he was seen only from the waist up.
9 (a) Presley's personal life suffered desperately, and he fought battles with weight gain and drug dependence.	(b) Desperately Presley's personal life suffered, and battles with weight gain and drug dependence he fought.
10 (a) Before Presley, there were no teenagers, just young people without a voice. He was one of the founders of youth culture.	(b) Teenagers were just young people without a voice before Presley. Youth culture was founded by people like him.

2 **T 12.6** Listen and check your answers.

3 Write about the career of someone who interests you. It could be a sportsperson,
  an artist, a singer, an actor, a writer, a business person … anybody!
  Get some facts and dates about the person – their early life, how their career grew,
  what the high points of their professional life were/have been.

PostScript

Linking and commenting

1 Look at these extracts from tapescript 12.5. The expressions in italics link or comment on what has been said or what is going to be said. They are mainly adverbs.

I think it *somehow sort of* gets rid of the values, *possibly,*

... that can be covering up, *you know,* feelings.

... the advent of the Pill was *obviously* a great event as well ...

... life *certainly* was different after it than before ...

Probably because things were coming to an end before it, *anyway* ...

For me *personally* ... the greatest moment of change in the twentieth century was *actually* Elvis Presley.

2 In these dialogues, choose the correct linking or commenting expression.

a A Did you see the match last night?
   B No, I missed it, but **apparently/obviously** it was a good game. We won, didn't we?
   A **Probably/Actually**, it was a draw, but it was really exciting.

b A What do you think of Claire's new boyfriend?
   B **Personally/Ideally**, I can't stand him. I think she'll be let down by him. **Certainly/However**, that's her problem, not mine.
   A Poor old Claire! She always picks the wrong ones, doesn't she? **Anyway/Honestly**, I'll see you later. Bye!
   B Bye, Rita.

c A I don't know how you can afford to buy all those fabulous clothes!
   B **Still /Hopefully**, I'm going to get a bonus this month. I should do. My boss promised it to me. **After all/Presumably**, I did earn the company over £100,000 last year. **Basically/Actually**, it was nearer £150,000. I do deserve it, don't you think?
   A **Of course/In fact** you do.

d A She said some horrible things to me. I hate her! She called me names!
   B **Generally speaking/All the same**, I think you should apologize to her.
   A Me? Apologize? Never!
   B **Basically/Surely**, I think you're both being very childish. Why don't you grow up?
   A Oh, Mary! **Still/Honestly**, I never thought you'd speak to me like that. I hate you, too.

e A So, Billy Peebles. You say that this is the last record you're ever going to make?
   B **Surely/Definitely**.
   A But **surely/actually** you realize how upset your fans are going to be?
   B **Obviously/As a matter of fact**, I don't want to hurt anyone, but **certainly/basically**, I'm fed up with pop music. I'd like to do something else. **After all/Ideally**, I'd like to get into films.
   A Well, we wish you all the best.

3 T12.7 Listen and check your answers. Practise the dialogues.

Tapescripts

UNIT 7

T7.1 See p 68

T7.2

Dear Sean

My dear Sean,
How lovely to get your letter! Mummy is right!
I will really enjoy helping you with your
schoolwork, and I will try very hard to
remember what it was like when I was a little girl
all those years ago.
When the war started, I was just five and I'll
never forget watching my grandfather dig a big
black hole in the back garden. This was our air
raid shelter. At first I was really scared of going
into it . Every time the siren went off, I started
trembling and I was sick, actually sick with fear.
I refused to leave my bed. I didn't find it easy to
get used to sleeping in that shelter. But soon,
living in the cities was so dangerous that the
government decided to send all the children
away to the countryside. I think I was lucky
because I was able to go away to my
grandmother's. Some children were forced to
stay with total strangers. My grandma lived in a
small town, called Alston, high in the hills, not
too far from Newcastle. And guess what Sean,
she had a sweet shop! Mrs Crozier's Sweet Shop.
But , oh dear me, at first I was so unhappy, I
couldn't stop crying because I couldn't help
worrying about my mother back home.
Grandma let me have as many sweets as I
wanted, but I was too miserable to eat many.
Silly me! Most children didn't have the chace of
getting lots of sweets because sweets were
rationed. That meant that you couldn't buy all
you wanted. You were only allowed to buy a
small amount. Lots of other things were
rationed, too. It was almost impossible to get
butter, cream, meat, fruit, vegetables and petrol.
We did without a lot of things during the war.
Can you believe that just after it ended someone
gave me a banana and I didn't know what to do
with it?
Sean, I hope this is useful. I'm longing to see
you all. Give my love to Mummy, Daddy and
Liam Don't worry, he'll be much more fun soon.

Lots of love and kisses
Grandma

T7.3

a A Are we going to have a break?
  B No, we don't have time to.

b A Can I smoke in here?
  B No, you're not allowed to.

c A I can't help you do your homework this
     evening. Sorry.
  B Oh, but you promised to!

d A Why did you do Exercise 2?
  B Because you told us to.

e A You said you'd phone me last night.
  B I'm really sorry, I meant to, but I forgot.

f A Have you finished marking the homework
     yet?
  B Sorry, I haven't had a chance to.

T7.4

a 'There's no way I'm going to give up using
   my car!'
b 'It's a beautiful morning, isn't it dear?'
c 'No, I haven't ironed your white shirt yet! I
   haven't had the time.'
d 'Come on! Stop gazing at that blank screen.
   Let's have a game of Scrabble.'
e 'Well, I'm not doing it! I did it last night.
   Anyway I want to mend the puncture on
   my bike.'
f 'Damn! I forgot to buy sugar!'
g 'If it were up to me, I'd throw the lot out!'
h 'Personally, I think life was much harder fifty
   years ago.'
i 'Never again! That was the longest three days
   of my life!'

T7.5

You've got a fast car
I want a ticket to anywhere
Maybe we (can) make a deal
Maybe together we can get somewhere
Any place is better
Starting from zero we've got nothing to lose
Maybe we'll make something
But me myself I've got nothing to prove.

You've got a fast car
And I've got a plan to get us out of here
I've been working at a convenience store
Managed to save just a little bit of money
We won't have to drive too far
Just cross the border and into the city
You and I can both get jobs
And finally see what it means to be living.

You see my old man's got a problem
He lives with the bottle, that's the way it is
He says his body's too old for working
His body's too young to look like his
My mama went off and left him
She wanted more from life than he could give
I said somebody's got to take care of him
So I quit school and that's what I did.

You've got a fast car
But is it fast enough so we can fly away?
We've got to make a decision
We leave tonight or live and die this way.

*I remember when we were driving driving in your
car*
The speed so fast I felt like I was drunk
City lights lay out before us
*And your arm felt nice wrapped round my
shoulder*
And I had a feeling that I belonged
*And I had a feeling I could be someone, be
someone, be someone.*

You've got a fast car
And we go cruising to entertain ourselves
You still ain't got a job
Now I work in a market as a checkout girl
I know things will get better
You'll find work and I'll get promoted
We'll move out of the shelter
Buy a bigger house and live in the suburbs.

I remember when ... etc.

You've got a fast car
And I've got a job that pays all our bills
You stay out drinking late at the bar
See more of your friends than you do of your
kids
I'd always hoped for better
Thought maybe together you and me would
find it
I've got no plans and I ain't going nowhere
So take your fast car and keep on driving.

I remember when ... etc.

You've got a fast car
But is it fast enough so you can fly away?
You've got to make a decision
You leave tonight or live and die this way.

T7.6

1
OK, folks. Don't go away now. We'll be back in
a few minutes, just after the break.

2
A It's not fair! Everyone else is allowed to go.
B I don't care about everyone else. You're not,
   and that's all there is to it.

3
A Open wide and say 'Ah'. Oh, dear.
B Ish it bad newsh?

4
A A big Mac with regular fries and a
   strawberry milkshake.
B Eat here or take away?

5
Mummy! I need a wee-wee!

6
Has Kelly Jones' latest album been released yet?

7
Well, I'm just going to put my feet up and have a
nap, if that's all right with you.

8
Let passengers off first. Move right down inside
the car.

9
Thanks for having me!

10
'scuse fingers!

11
A With respect to my Right Honourable friend,
   I have to say that I find his statement to be
   inconsistent with the truth.
B Ooh!
C Hear, hear!

12

A Things aren't what they used to be.
B You can say that again. It was different in our day, wasn't it?

13

Will passengers in rows A to K please board now?

14

A I can't find my gym kit.
B Think. Where did you last have it?

15

News is coming in of a major hold-up on the A45 Colchester bypass. Drivers are advised to avoid this area if at all possible.

16

A Could you develop this for me?
B Normal six by four?
A Yeah, that's fine.
B When do you want them by?
A This time tomorrow's all right.

UNIT 8

T8.1 See p 80

T8.2

R = Rod   M = Miranda

R Hello. Kingsbridge 810344. Rod speaking.
M Hi, Rod. It's me, Miranda. I've got to talk to you.
R Oh, hi Miranda. Why all the excitement?
M Well, can you remember that competition I entered, just for a laugh, a few weeks ago?
R Yes, I can. I remember you doing it in the coffee bar. It was the one in the *Daily Express*, wasn't it? Didn't you have to name loads of capital cities?
M Yes, that's it. You've got it. Well, get this, I've won it! I came first!
R You can't have! I don't believe it! What's the prize?
M A trip to New York.
R You must be kidding! That's brilliant. For how long?
M Just three days – but it's three days in the Waldorf Astoria, of all places!
R Well, you should be able to do quite a lot in three days. And the Waldorf Astoria! I'm impressed! Isn't that on Park Avenue?
M Yes, it is.
R I thought so. Not that I've been there of course.
M And Rod, there's something else, even better than that.
R And what could possibly be even better than that?
M Well, you won't believe it ... but the journey there and back is on Concorde!
R Wow! That's fantastic. That's something I've always wanted to do. D'you know it only takes three and a half hours, so you arrive before you've left ..., if you see what I mean.
M I know. And another thing Rod. It's a trip for two and I'd really love it if you would

come with me. Will you?
R You can't be serious? You know I'd love to! But why me? Surely you should be taking Richard.
M Haven't you heard? Richard and I have split up. You must have known it had been going wrong between us for ages.
R Oh, sorry! I didn't know. I really am sorry. When did this happen?
M Well, a couple of weeks ago. We ...

T8.3

a A Oh no! I've lost my passport.
   B Well, you could have left it in the taxi.
   A Oh, thank goodness! Here it is at the bottom of my bag.

b A It's an early start for us tomorrow.
   B Really? What time do we have to set off?
   A Well, the taxi's arriving at six o'clock. We have to be at the airport at seven.

c A The traffic's not moving. We'll never get to the concert.
   B Don't worry, don't worry. We should still be there in plenty of time.
   A But I'd hate to miss the beginning.

d A I've brought you some flowers. I hope you like tulips.
   B Oh, how kind of you, you needn't have. I love all spring flowers.
   A I thought you might.

e A All the teachers are going on strike!
   B What? That's brilliant, we don't have to come to school tomorrow.
   A The bad news is that they're setting us loads of homework!

T8.4

A That film was very good, wasn't it?
B Good? It was absolutely fantastic!

A You must have been quite pleased when you passed your exam.
B Pleased? I was absolutely delighted!

T8.5

The Oscar ceremony

'I am absolutely delighted to receive this award, and I am sincerely grateful to all those wonderful people who voted for me. *Kisses and Dreams* was a fantastic movie to work on from start to finish. And I thank all those brilliant and talented people involved in the making of this absolutely fantastic film. Nobody could have possibly known that it would be such a huge success, especially those who told us at the start that the plot was boring and ridiculous. They have now been proved quite wrong. My particular thanks go to Marius Aherne my marvellous director; Julietta Brioche my gorgeous co-star; Roger Sims for writing such a hilarious and thrilling story. I absolutely adore you all.'

T8.6

[two extracts from musicals]

T8.7

I = Interviewer   TR = Tim Rice

I I went to interview Tim Rice in his London home by the Thames, and we discussed how he came to create a musical about a religious figure.
I What a subject to choose! Why did you choose to write about Jesus Christ?
TR In a way I guess it's rather an obvious subject, I mean so many people have written versions of the Jesus story, whether it be in serious music, straight plays, movies and in our case pop music or rock music. And I can't really remember why, other than the fact that when I was at school, and I went to a school that placed a great emphasis on religion and going to chapel, the character of Judas Iscariot always intrigued me, because here was a guy who was central to the whole Jesus story, without him there wouldn't be much of a story, if he hadn't betrayed Jesus, and yet the sketch of him in the Bible is just that. And the idea of Judas Iscariot seemed to be rather a good one, but of course once we got into it, once I began drafting out the story line as seen from Judas's point of view it became clear that really the piece should be called *Jesus Christ* or as it became *Jesus Christ Superstar* because Jesus is the most important character by far.
I But how did he come to decide on the term 'superstar'?
TR It was ... originally that song was just *Jesus Christ, Jesus Christ, who are you? What have you sacrificed?* And I can remember working in my parents' house, and it was one Sunday morning before lunch and I thought 'Gosh! Superstar, da da dum, ba ba bom', and I just put it in and it seemed to work.
I I then asked Tim if he was surprised by the reaction of certain church people who hammered him for it, and hammered the show for being too simplistic, even blasphemous?
TR Well, I suppose we were surprised by the fact that it was noticed at all. When we wrote it ... erm ... we didn't really contemplate what reaction it would have with the world outside because, certainly I didn't ever think it would hit the world outside. I thought ... well, this is quite good but other people have hits, this ... this isn't the sort of thing that's going to be known ... erm ... and then when it did come out and particularly in America, when it was a huge overnight smash on record, we then did get some reaction, but the reaction that surprised me more was the churchmen who quickly took it up as ... as a thing to help their congregations, their causes. I remember going to one church service in New York and seeing a baby being christened in the name of Jesus Christ Superstar.

T8.8

I = Interviewer   PN = Paul Nicholas

The actor, Paul Nicholas, played the part of Jesus in the first-ever production.

I   What do you think it was in the show that made it so successful?

PN   Well I think the subject was somewhat taboo therefore it made it sort of slightly risky and interesting ... er ... I think from their point of view they were young when they wrote it, Andrew and Tim, and therefore had the courage to write lyrics that were perhaps a little near the knuckle and music that certainly was, was ... very strong and youthful and brave.

I   It must have been a bit strange for you to suddenly be in this part of Jesus.

PN   No, I think, I think the strange part for me was playing such a recognizable figure ... er ... a figure that meant so much to so many people and trying to do it justice for them and in some ways it was very moving. I remember the first time that ... we did the crucifixion, and I went up on the cross and there's a wonderful piece of music that Andrew played, or composed at that point, which I was very overcome with ... with the vulnerability of actually hanging there on a cross with this music going on, and it made me cry, I remember ... erm ... but thereafter ... after eight performances a week for about two or three weeks it became like a job, and most of the time I ... I was more concerned that I may sneeze ... in ... while I was up on the cross, which would have slightly ruined the evening for ... for many people. Indeed the problem for me with the show was that there weren't really enough laughs ... er the only time I managed to crack a joke was, I remember at the beginning of the second act, a gentleman in the front row sneezed, and I couldn't resist saying 'God bless you my son' which was ... I realized about that point that perhaps it was time I moved on.

I   Say you were playing the part now ... erm how would you be different from twenty-five years ago?

PN   If I were playing it ... erm ... I think I'd do probably much the same thing as I did before but probably better. I'd probably sing better, I would understand it better. The only thing is I probably wouldn't ... wouldn't look as slim on the cross! If the truth be known.

T8.9

a   A   I'm starving. I could eat a horse.
    B   Yes, I'm a little peckish, too.

b   A   I'm absolutely dying for a drink.
    B   Yes, my throat's a bit dry, I must say.

c   A   His family are pretty well off, aren't they?
    B   You can say that again. They're absolutely loaded!

d   A   You must have hit the roof when she told you she'd crashed your car.
    B   Well, yes, I was a bit upset.

e   A   I think Tony was a bit tipsy last night.
    B   What! He was totally smashed out of his brain!

f   A   I can't stand the sight of him.
    B   I must admit, I'm not too keen on him, either.

g   A   He isn't very bright, is he?
    B   You're not kidding. He's as thick as two short planks.

h   A   Look at the weather! It's vile again.
    B   I know. It is a bit wet, but we mustn't grumble, must we?

i   A   What a fantastic holiday!
    B   Yes, it was a nice little break, but all good things must come to an end.

j   A   I'm knackered. Can we stop for a rest?
    B   OK. I feel a bit out of breath, too.

k   A   He invited quite a few friends to his party.
    B   I'll say. We had to fight our way through millions of people to get to the drinks.

l   A   Well, that journey was absolute hell!
    B   I suppose it did take rather a long time to get here.

m   A   They've got this huge great dog called Wizzer. I'm terrified of it.
    B   What? That little thing wouldn't hurt a fly!

UNIT 9

T9.1

1   I'm not really going babysitting. I just don't want to go out with Mark. I can't stand him. I don't know why he keeps asking me to go out with him. If he rings again, I'm not in, right?

2   I didn't actually trip over the cat. I was in a fight. I can't even remember what it was all about.

3   It's awful! It doesn't suit her at all! I don't know why she bought it.

4   I'm not going to Laura's to watch telly. I'm going out with a bloke called Max. I daren't tell my Dad about him 'cos he's 25. I think my Dad would kill me if he knew.

5   Actually, I hate being at college. I haven't made any friends and I'm really homesick, but I don't want to upset Mum and Dad.

6   I'm not ill at all. I just want a day off work. I'm going to play golf.

7   Miss Jones isn't out of the office. She's sitting right there, but she doesn't want to be disturbed at the moment.

T9.2

a   Who did she give her money away to?
b   What do you want to have a word with me about?
c   Who did you dance with?

d   What do you need £5,000 for?
e   What's he writing a book about?
f   Who did you get a present from?
g   Who did you buy a birthday card for?
h   What are you thinking about?
i   Where do you want me to give you a lift to?
j   What do you want me to clean the sink with?

T9.3   See p 90

T9.4   See p 90

T9.5

a   Don't you think it's time to go home?
b   Can't they understand what they have to do?
c   Aren't you coming to the cinema with us?
d   Hasn't she ever been abroad?
e   Isn't that Peter sitting over there?
f   Haven't I met you somewhere before?
g   Hasn't the postman been yet?
h   Weren't you in my class at school?
i   Didn't you want to watch the football tonight?

T9.6

This is Radio 4. This week in 'File on Life': *Saying 'I won't'* or *What stopped the wedding?* The photographer may be booked, the cake may be iced, and the dress may fit perfectly, but suddenly it's all off. What stops the wedding and forces one half of the happy couple into saying 'I won't'? Listen to the stories of Elizabeth, George, and Nicole.

Elizabeth

The nearer it got to the date, there ... there was more pressure. I felt more and more pressure on me because everybody'd been out and bought their wedding gear and I'd had the final fitting for the dress. It was ivory, and everyone said how great it looked. And ... and ... the printing of the stationery'd been done and the cake'd been made. There was so much pressure and it was awful 'cos deep down inside I knew ... I knew it was wrong. But the pressure was to go through with it just for the sake of keeping everyone happy. I felt inside ... I can't, I can't, I can't go through with this, but I've got to because of all the expense ... I mean the cost of everything. The whole thing was confused in my head. In the end I tried to say something to my mum, but she kept saying 'Come on, it's just nerves'. She said she'd felt the same before marrying dad, they all said it was just nerves, but I knew ... I knew it wasn't. I knew I had to pluck up courage and speak out ... it, it wasn't fair on anybody, 'specially Paul. I just didn't love him any more. We'd been going out since we were sixteen. Kids really. He was like my brother.

Afterwards it was such relief, it was like a cork coming out of a bottle. It all just poured out. Paul was upset, yes, of course he was, but not distraught, not really. Not as much as I'd thought anyway. It was my little sister, she was distraught, 'cos she had the dress and was going to be bridesmaid and everything. I felt worse for her ... terrible. But in fact my family were brilliant ... er ... in the end, and actually we wore the dresses, me and my sister, we went to a fancy dress party, yes, we went as the brides of Frankenstein! Wasn't that awful?

George

It was the rehearsal. We had a rehearsal a week before the wedding. Everything was fine. Vicky and I went to the church and we met the best man and the bridesmaids ... and it was all fine. And we went through the ceremony and, and we were all very happy and everything was fine and then ... then, it was just sort of after that, and we had to fill in some forms and we were all sitting down and filling in the forms and then, Vicky, she couldn't fill the forms in, and she had this ... er ... panic attack. She was just sitting down crying and screaming and saying 'I can't do it, I just can't do it, I can't face it'. I was just sitting there holding her hand really, comforting her. At that point I think I was more concerned for her really, rather than for me. I was upset that she was upset and I said ... in the end ... I said to her and to the minister that maybe it would be better to postpone it. And then ... then it was amazing, just amazing. From the moment she knew the wedding was off she was perfectly normal and the relationship was perfectly normal. In fact a week later on the actual day when we should have been getting married, we went for a drive by the lake and it was a super hot day, and we had a picnic and it was a really smashing day. I really enjoyed it. I don't think we'll ever marry now ... not to each other anyway.

Nicole

I was just getting out of the white Rolls Royce. I was sitting in my wedding dress outside a Greek cathedral in downtown Manhattan. And then, then suddenly someone came out of the church, I dunno who this guy was, but he thrust a piece of paper in my hand and ran. I didn't know what it was, I opened it, and read it ... seven words, just seven words and the end of my world! It said 'I can't go through with it. Michael.' Can you believe it? Not even '*Love* Michael'. I was in shock. I ... felt ... it felt like I was in a movie. So I thought, 'What would they do in a movie?' And I figured ...er ... I could see it all in my head, so I got out of the car and I went into the church ... it was packed. I just went in and I walked slowly down the aisle, all by myself, like in slow-motion, then I turned and ... it was real dramatic ... I announced, 'Michael's not coming but let's have a party anyway.' So that's what we did. I had a non-wedding reception. It was spectacular. I'm afraid I got pretty drunk ... very drunk in fact. All I can remember is dancing non-stop to 'I Will Survive'. *I will survive, oooh yeah I will survive.*

I haven't heard a word from him since that note. I think I'm angrier now than I was then. I just want him to tell me, in person, why he did this to me. He could at least tell me the reason. He's a sh ... shameful human being. I can't

believe he's the same man I met last year on that beach in Greece. We talked the same language, we had so much in common. You see, we're both Greek, at least our parents are Greek, but he was born and raised in London and I was born in New York. Last March he proposed to me on the telephone. I was in heaven. I just believed he was my destiny.

You know, I spent $25,000 on this wedding and he wasn't even there. I've kept the ring, it cost $6,000. The dress cost $2,000. No, I don't know where he is now. It wouldn't surprise me if he'd gone to Tahiti where we'd planned to have our honeymoon. Actually nothing would surprise me. Maybe he's already married. Who cares?

T9.7

There was I waiting at the church, waiting at the church, waiting at the church,
When I found he'd left me in the lurch.
Lor, how it did upset me!
All at once he sent me round a note.
Here's the very note, this is what he wrote,
'Can't get away to marry you today. My wife won't let me!'

I'm in a nice bit of trouble, I confess.
Somebody with me has had a game.
I should by now be a proud and happy bride,
But I've still got to keep my single name.
I was proposed to by Obadiah Binks
In a very gentlemanly way.
Lent him all my money so that he could buy a home,
And punctually at twelve o' clock today,

There was I waiting at the church, waiting at the church, waiting at the church,
When I found he'd left me in the lurch.
Lor, how it did upset me!
All at once he sent me round a note.
Here's the very note, this is what he wrote,
'Can't get away to marry you today. My wife won't let me!'

T9.8

a 1 I'm sorry to bother you, but could you possibly change a five-pound note?
2 Have you got change for a five-pound note?

b 1 Where's the station?
2 Could you tell me where the station is, please?

c 1 A This is a present for you.
B For me! Oh, how kind! You shouldn't have, really. Thank you so much.
2 C This is a present for you.
D Thanks.

d 1 A Can you come to a party on Saturday?
B No, I can't.
2 C Can you come to a party on Saturday?
D Oh, what a pity! I'm already going out, I'm afraid.
C Never mind!
D Thanks for the invitation.

e 1 A Excuse me! Do you mind if I sit down here?
B No, not at all.
2 C Is anyone sitting here?
D No.

f 1 A You forgot to post my letter.
B Sorry.
2 C You've spilt red wine on my dress!
D I am SO sorry. I do apologize, Madam. I don't know how it happened. Let me get a cloth.

g 1 A Can you give me a hand? I need to carry this box upstairs.
B OK.
2 C I wonder if I could possibly ask you a favour? You see, I need to get this box upstairs. Would you mind helping me?
D No, not at all.

h 1 A So I said ...
B Pardon? What was that?
2 C So I said ...
D What?

i 1 A Goodbye. It was a lovely evening. Thank you so much. We had a wonderful time.
B We enjoyed it, too. So glad you could make it. Safe journey back. See you soon.
C Bye.
D Good night. Take care.
2 E Goodbye. Thanks for the meal.
F Bye. See you.

T9.9

a A Hi! Listen, can you come round for a meal tomorrow evening? I'm cooking Chinese.

b A Can you help me with my maths homework? We're doing algebra.

c A Would you like me to babysit this evening so you can go out for a meal?

d A Can you tell me where the nearest post office is, please?

e A Hi, it's Susan here. Could I ask you a big favour? Could you look after my dog next week? I have to go away.

T9.10

a A Hi! Listen, can you come round for a meal tomorrow evening? I'm cooking Chinese.
B Oh, I'd love to, but I'm afraid I'm already going out. Oh, what a shame!

b A Can you help me with my maths homework? We're doing algebra.
B Believe me, I would if I could, but I don't know the first thing about algebra. Sorry.

c A Would you like me to babysit this evening so you can go out for a meal?
B That's very kind of you, but we've arranged for my sister to come over. Thanks for the offer, though.

d A Can you tell me where the nearest post office is, please?

B I'm afraid I don't know. Sorry.

e A Hi, it's Susan here. Could I ask you a big favour? Could you look after my dog next week? I have to go away.

B I'm terribly sorry, Susan, but I can't. I'd love to have Molly, you know I adore dogs, but I'm going away myself for a few days.

T9.11

A and B = Hostess and Host   H = Henry

A Pat! Hello! How lovely to see you. Come on in. Let me take your coat.
– *Give the flowers to your host.*

A How kind of you! They're lovely. Thank you so much. Now, do you know everybody? Let me introduce you to Henry. Henry, this is Pat.

H Hello, Pat. Nice to meet you.

—

H Where are you from, Pat?

—

H That's interesting. And what are you doing in London?

—

H And how do you find London, Pat? Is it like home, or is it very different?

—

A Now, Pat. What would you like to drink?

—

A Right. I'll just get that for you.

B Pat, do have some nuts.

—

A Right, everybody. Dinner's ready. Come and sit down. Pat, you sit here next to me.

—

B Has everyone got a drink? Cheers, everybody!

—

A Pat, help yourself. Would you like some roast parsnips?

—

A Roast parsnips. It's a vegetable. Maybe you don't have them in your country. Would you like to try some?

—

A Pat, what about some more to eat?

B Another glass of wine, perhaps?

B I hope you enjoyed your meal, Pat.

—

A Well, Pat. We're so glad you could come. It's a shame you have to leave so early.

—

B Thank you, Pat. Safe journey back. Bye now!

UNIT 10

T10.1

Rosemary Sage is 100 years old. She lives in the village of Hambledon, Surrey. Many people commute daily from Hambledon to work in London. Rosemary has only been to London once in her life, when she went to the zoo sixty years ago!

Her daily routine goes back to a time before there were any commuters in the village. It never varies. At the start of each day, she gathers and chops wood for the fire, on which she'll boil a large kettle of water. Then she'll carry some of the water to her wash-house in the garden and she'll get washed. Next she'll make herself a cup of tea. She has no means of heating or cooking apart from the open fire. Her home is like a working museum, and her clear memory is a precious source of knowledge of old country ways. She's always telling stories of when she was young.

In those days, the Lord and Lady of the Manor used to own all the cottages and they rented them to the villagers for 2s 9d (14p) a week. Every winter the village pond would freeze over and she'd go skating with her six brothers and sisters. Every summer they'd spend one day at the seaside. Other than that and her one trip to London, she has hardly ever left the village. She is perfectly content with her life. She has no bath, no fridge, and no telephone. 'I could never get used to such 'modern' appliances at my age,' she says. 'I'm used to the old ways. I'm far too old to change.'

T10.2

My first friend? Well, … I suppose my first *best* friend was when I was about eight. It was a girl in our street. She lived up the road in a big white house, … er … it was a much bigger house than ours. We went to the same school but we didn't use to see much of each other at school 'cos we were in different classes. She was a bit older than me. Oh, … her name … she was … oh, Gillian Milne. Her dad had a really good job with the local brewery. I suppose we had a lot in common but we used to fight a lot, too. We both loved going to the cinema, 'specially to see musicals. We'd learn all the words of the songs by heart, and we'd come home and we'd act it all out in the field at the end of the road. Yuk! I mean it sounds really nauseating now! But I have to say it seemed really good fun at the time, … but then we were always having these huge rows about nothing. You see, I used to think that she was spoilt rotten. Honestly, she just got everything she wanted. When the ice-cream van came round she'd get four flavours *and* an ice lolly and she was so mean. She wouldn't share a thing, and she'd just burst into tears and run home to mummy! Actually, when I think of it now, I'm not really sure why we were friends. Oh, I once went on holiday to Blackpool with her and her Auntie Ethel and it was a disaster.

T10.3

a How often do you get homework?
Well, we usually get it twice a week.

b Do you read many books in English?
Well, yes, I do now, but I didn't use to.

c Do you find it easy to use your monolingual dictionary?
I didn't at first, but I soon got used to it.

d Do you look up every word that you can't understand?
Well, I don't now, but I used to when I was a beginner.

e How can you understand English when it is spoken so quickly?
Well, I suppose I'm used to it.

f Did you do much pronunciation practice when you were first learning English?
Oh, yes we did. We used to do it every lesson.

g How do you find using the telephone in English?
It's not easy, but I think that gradually I'm getting used to it.

T10.4

Part 1

O = Oliver McGechy   I = Interviewer

I Hello, and welcome to 'Worldly Wise'. In today's edition, we look at the problem of homelessness.
Why is it that, even in the richest countries in the world, there are so many homeless people? Someone who has experienced the problem first hand, as a homeless person himself, is Oliver McGechy, a former journalist and publisher and a reformed alcoholic. He now works to help others in the same position.
I asked Oliver if he could tell us something about the work he does, and the problems of homeless people.

O I run a project for people who have a long-term commitment to alcohol recovery and who basically are homeless and … er … who … who need help. It was put to me the other day that in Europe at the moment that the average lifespan is for someone who's street homeless is only 42. So you're actually moving back to almost Victorian days and Victorian principles in terms of how people can expect to live and what quality of life they can expect. But the people you see sleeping on the streets, the people you see sleeping in … in shop doorways represent only the tip of the iceberg, they represent … represent only a very, very small proportion of the … the overall number of people, who … who are actually homeless.

I I asked Oliver what had gone wrong in these people's lives.

O You're looking at someone who's not only lost their home, they've probably lost their partner, their children, their family, all of the social contact which they've had … they've probably lost all of the network which has supported them within society, their doctors ... their GP, ... erm their dentist, their job. They become unemployed, and because they're into a downward spiral all of these things combine to make it very, very difficult to move back into society. Therefore they become lost. They tend to be forgotten. There's little political gain in supporting homeless people.

I Who exactly are these people, Oliver?

O It ... it's impossible to say. I mean ... I've worked with people who have been accountants, I've worked with people who have been doctors, I've worked with a number of members of the clergy ... erm ... I've worked with people who have worked in factories, I've worked with people who have never worked in their life at all. I've worked with postmen, I've worked with ex-service men. The spread of people who ... who are affected by homelessness, or who have become homeless, is ... is infinite, is as wide as society itself.

I But are there problems that all of these people have in common?

O One of the biggest problems which homeless people face in fact is drug addiction and alcoholism, but let me ask you a question. If you were homeless and you had nowhere to live, and you'd lost your family, you'd lost your job, ... life had fallen round ... er fallen down roundabout you, and you could escape just a little by using alcohol, would you?

I Absolutely ... I take the point.

Part 2

C = Chris Caine

I Chris, can you tell us why it was that you ended up homeless?

C Well, I 'ad a house wiv a woman that I ... er took on, wiv 'er kids and I 'ad a job 'n' all, workin' at the Royal Mail Post Office ... erm I dunno about .. ... what ... two, two years it was into the relationship and all of a sudden, like, she just wanted out, so ... er I tried to patch 'fings up which really didn't work, yer know, so I ended up going back to the woods, well, yer know, where I was before ...

I Back to the woods?

C Yeah.

I How d'you mean? Literally to the woods?

C Yeah. I used to lived out in the woods.

I Did you?

C Yeah.

I What ... er .. you mean ... living rough (Yeah, living rough in the woods) or in a tent, or how?

C Just in a 'bivvy' bag, Goretex 'bivvy' bag, 'n' sleeping bag and stuff, in the woods, for a while, lighting fires 'n' havin' my grub out there, yer know. There's just summink about the woods .. yer free out there ... you, yer can't do it round the towns 'cos there's ... you know ... erm ... you're too at risk in towns, too many people ... yer know ... too much ... too much hassle in towns. Best fing to do is get out and, and get ... get where you feel safe, so I feel safe in the woods all the time

yer know ... erm ...

I So why aren't you in the woods now?

C 'Cos I 'ad a breakdown out there, and I went to the doctor's 'n' that and he give me some tablets for that, and I ended up comin' here ... was the best solution ... yer know ... to ... er ... get meself back on my feet ... sort of thing ... yer know.

I But ... so living in the woods, although as you say ... it was ... you know, you were free, free from the hassles and so on, I mean ... it's not the ideal way of life for you?

C Erm ... no and yes. It was my job once ... (upon) a time.

I Living in the woods?

C Yeah, I was a survival instructor, teaching the army and stuff.

I So you like the woods?

C ... the woods, the mountains is fine for me. But coming into towns I find very stressful ... erm I'm here now but each time, here now, I'm still fightin'. I've been here six months, so each day now I'm still fighting to stay here, which is hard for me ... I'd be safe out there, yer know, instead of here, but ... all I'm trying to do is get me act togever and start again really. It's ... it's hard work.

I What does it mean to you not to have a home?

C Devastating, really. I miss the family feeling or the family comfort, not ... not the television but having a woman there to care for, and someone to talk to. You get very lonely. I mean, in here you've got friends 'n' 'at ... but I admit I get very lonely when you're on your own, an' it takes its toll because if you're used to that way of life, it's hard to comprehend what it's all about ... yer know the worst fing is, when yer think about that which hurts most, is to see people holding hands going down the street with their wife and kids and you've had that once and you've lost it, and you'd like that again but it's going to take time to get that back ... yer know so ... erm, yeah I find it really hard, actually.

I And what's it like when you're actually on the road?

C When yer roamin' round the country yer see so many of yer people like yerself ... erm on the street, sleepin' in doorways, parks, benches, yer know, and ... erm yeah, yer kind of get used to it after a while, it takes about a week to get used to being on the road but then it takes about seven ... seven to eight months trying to get used to getting back into society again, you know. I find it hard anyway, even now.

Part 3

I Chris is just one of a growing army of people of all ages and positions in life who have become homeless and have ended up sleeping rough. Throughout the ages there have always been homeless people. For some, a life without obligations and responsibilities has its attractions. But, for most homeless people, like Chris, the everyday world of

homelessness is very grim indeed.

C Well, when you get to rock bottom, you either turn yourself to drink or drugs. An' you can get drunk as much as you want but the next day it's still there. You got the same problem as you did the day before.

UNIT 11

T11.1

a I wish I lived somewhere warm, preferably the Mediterranean, and ideally the island of Gozo, near Malta.

b If only I weren't such a quick-tempered person. If I hadn't shouted at George the other day, we'd still be friends.

c I wish I could read faster, 'cos there's so many books I want to read and there's never enough time, 'cept when you're on holiday. I wish I had longer holidays, but I still wouldn't get through them all.

d If only animals could talk, I'd be able to really know what our dogs think of us.

e If only I hadn't parked my car on the double yellow line I wouldn't have got that ticket. I knew it was a mistake ... it was a very busy Saturday and the traffic wardens are often out on the High Street, but I thought, well, if I just park it round here, just round the corner, just off the main High Street, I'm sure that I'll be OK, it's only for twenty minutes.

f I wish I'd listened to my grandmother more before she died. She was full of stories about all kinds of weird and wonderful people in our family. And now ... now, I'm trying to draw up our family tree, so you see I'd be really interested in it all.

g I wish I hadn't studied business and politics at university. I should have studied languages, I'd love to be able to speak French and Spanish fluently. But if I hadn't studied politics ... I suppose ... I might never have met Andy.

h I shouldn't have eaten that huge slice of chocolate cake last night. I'm going to Tenerife in two months' time, and I want to try and lose weight so I can wear my bikini.

T11.2 See p 109

T11.3

1 If only you'd told me earlier.

2 I wish you'd help more with the housework.

3 I wish you'd helped me with my homework.

4 I'd have passed the exam if you'd helped me.

5 If you'd turned left not right, we'd be there by now.

6 She'd come if he weren't coming.

7 If she'd come, I'd have introduced you to her.

8 I'd rather you'd asked me before you'd written to complain.

T11.4

P = Peter   A = Amanda

P Hello, Amanda.

A Peter!

P I'm surprised you recognize me.

A Really? You haven't moved back here, have you?

P Good heavens no ... erm ... I'm still in London. I came back for the funeral. My father's. A heart attack. It happened very suddenly.

A I'm sorry.

P Thank you. And I take it that you're not living back here either?

A No, I'm in London, too, just back for my sister's wedding tomorrow.

P That's nice.

A Yes.

P And ... er ... your parents? They're well?

A Fine.

P Er ... are you rushing off somewhere?

A No, I'm just killing time, really.

P Then I suggest we kill it together. Let's grab a coffee.

A Er . . . and so, Peter, did you become a foreign correspondent?

P Not exactly. I'm a lawyer, believe it or not.

A You enjoy it?

P Yes. And you? Are you a world famous artist?

A Well ... er ... no.

P So. What are you up to?

A Nothing much. I've tried a few things.

P So you're not painting at all?

A Only doors and walls. So ... where are you in London?

P North. And you?

A South. It's okay, I rent a room, but I'm thinking of buying somewhere. It's one of the reasons I came home. I want to sort things out a bit. Oh, Peter, I don't know why I left that day.

P It's all right. We were young. Young people do things like that all the time.

A I suppose you're right. Well, ... I ... I ought to be going.

P Already? I thought you had time to kill.

A I did, ... but I ought to get back now to help my mother with the wedding.

P I understand. Shall I give you my phone number. Perhaps we could meet up?

A Perhaps. Thanks. Er ... goodbye, Peter.

P Goodbye, Amanda.

T11.5

Part one

My grandfather was not a black sheep in the sense that he was ... erm ... sent away by his family but he was rather a naughty man ... erm ... he was a silk dealer in Japan, and ... erm ... I'm trying to think of ... well the early part of this century and as was the custom with European families in Japan, they had servants in the family and my grandfather had an affair with the maid of the household, and, from that affair a daughter was born, and in fact unlike many black sheep my grandfather took responsibility for the ... the his offspring, and kept her in the house and in the family and in fact made sure that she had an education. And when his wife eventually died ... erm ... he did marry this Japanese maid ... erm ... I found out about this story through my mother who was in her teens at the time that the baby was born and of course was still alive and living at home when her mother died and when her father married again. And, it was obviously something very distressing for my mother because she had never mentioned it to me or any of my sisters until one dramatic day when her sister-in-law at the dinner table, with us present, asked my mother if she'd ever heard from Yuri, and we innocently asked 'Who is Yuri?' And this tale came out. I think it took my mother a long time to forgive her sister-in-law for this indiscretion. The indiscretion was totally innocent my ... my aunt had no idea that we were in the dark about this or that my mother was so sensitive about it but ... erm ... the interesting follow-up for me was that when I went to Japan about sixteen years ago, with my husband, my mother's step-sister, half-sister was actually living in Japan at that time having married a Swiss businessman, who had business in Japan. So I met my ... I call her my half-aunt, and I even met her mother who was still alive living in Tokyo, and the amazing thing for me was to go to a country as foreign as Japan and find that I actually had Japanese family as a result of the ... the black sheep adventures of my grandfather.

Part two

This is the main story in my family, actually ... erm ... it's the story of my great aunt's birth. She was born in Winnipeg, in 1900, in December, on December 13th and ... when ... she was born at home, and when she was born she was blue and wasn't breathing ... and the midwife said to the mother, 'Well, I'm ... I'm terribly sorry, there's nothing that we can do about this ... erm ... the child isn't breathing.' And the grandmother, who was present at the birth, said, 'Stuff and nonsense! Give me that child!' And she grabbed the baby, and she went downstairs, and she opened the door to the oven of the wood stove and she put my great aunt in the oven. And lo and behold a few minutes later a great cry came from the oven and my great aunt had been born. And my great aunt is still alive and is still able to tell this story.

T11.6

a A So why didn't you hand it in on time? I'm not going to mark it now.

   B But, I'm really sorry. I just didn't have the chance to finish it at the weekend.

b A It's always the same. I hummed and hawed about getting it, then when I went back it had been sold and it was one of his best works.

   B You should have asked if you could put a deposit on it.

c A Ouch! I've had it with this thing. It just doesn't work.

   B Here, give it to me! Let me try.

d A It's not fair. I'd been looking forward to watching it all day and then the phone goes and rings!

   B And who was it? Anyone interesting?

e A How many times do I have to tell you? Take them off before you come into the house!

   B Sorry. I forgot. I was in a hurry.

f A This has gone beyond a joke. You promised you'd deliver it by Tuesday at the latest. Now you're saying next month!

   B I'm awfully sorry, sir. I'm afraid there's nothing I can do about it.

g A I could kick myself. As soon as I'd handed in the paper, I remembered what the answer was.

   B But do you think you've still passed?

h A Of course, they didn't have it in red. Apparently, it only comes in navy blue.

   B But wouldn't that go well with your white jeans?

i A It's the last time I'll eat here.

   B You're not kidding! Massive prices and lousy food!

UNIT 12

T12.1

A Who gave you that new car?

B Susan gave it to me.

A Did she sell it to you?

B No, she gave it to me.

A Did she give it to Peter?

B No, she gave it to me.

A Is it second-hand?

B No, it's new.

A Did she give you a new stereo?

B No, she gave me a new car.

T12.2

a Did Ann give James a blue shirt?
   Did she give him a white shirt?
   Did she give him a blue jumper?
   Was it a Christmas present?

b Did James fly to Rome?
   Did he go to Paris by Eurostar?
   Did he want to do some shopping in Paris?
   Did he go there just for the weekend?

c Do you go to Scotland in summer?
   Do you go to Ireland in the autumn?
   Do you go there to relax?

d Is your daughter at Bristol university?
   Is it your youngest son that's studying at Bristol?
   Is he studying modern languages?

T12.3

a A Why weren't you at school yesterday?
   B I was at school.

b A Come on, Dave. Its time to get up.
   B I am getting up.

c A It's a shame you don't like parties.
   B But I do like parties!

d A I wish you'd tidy your room.
   B I have tidied it.

e A What a shame you didn't see Tom.
   B I did see Tom.

T12.4

1 How do you keep cool at a football match?
   Sit next to a fan.

2 Why do Swiss cows have bells?
   Because their horns don't work.

3 Customer: Waiter, waiter! I'm in a hurry.
              Will my pancake be long?
   Waiter: No, sir. It'll be round.

4 Mother: You spend too much money.
              Money doesn't grow on trees, you
              know.
   Daughter: Well, why do banks have so many
              branches, then?

5 What's the difference between a sailor and someone who goes shopping?
   One goes to sail the seas, the other goes to see the sales.

6 What's the difference between a jeweller and a jailer?
   One sells watches and the other watches cells.

7 What did the sea say to the beach?
   Nothing. It just waved.

8 What sort of crisps can fly?
   Plain crisps.

9 A prisoner is locked in a cell with only a chair. How does he escape?
   He rubs his hands until they are sore, he uses the saw to cut the chair in half. Two halves make a whole. He climbs through the hole and shouts himself hoarse. Then he gets on the horse and gallops away.

T12.5

Pam
For me, one of the most special moments of the twentieth century was the end of apartheid in South Africa, which I watched as much as possible on television, and I have a marvellous image in my mind of the morning Nelson Mandela was released, and he walked, as it were, to freedom, with Winnie by his side, and there were crowds of wonderfully excited people. It was a very moving moment.

David
I think the collapse of the Berlin Wall was one of the seminal events of the twentieth century. Er ... it led to erm ... an astonishingly fast collapse of communism across East Europe, the Soviet Union ... well, it didn't lead to it, but it all happened very, very quickly after that. So

we had er ... a social system, a political system which had covered large parts of the ... of the world, erm ... over a period of fifty or sixty years erm ... and then within the space of two or three years it had gone and what ... been ... sort of washed away, and erm ... led to erm ... the introduction of ... of capitalism erm ... good or bad, but it all happened incredibly quickly. So it has to count as one of the great events, human events as well as political events, of the twentieth century.

Alexa
Oh, I think that the Internet has changed erm ... quite a lot of people's perspective of the world. You can have conversations ... decent conversations with people from Australia, from America. And it's ... it's quite strange. Erm ... there is the thing, though, that the people you are talking to may not be the people they seem, I mean, they can lie about their age, what they look like. They even lie about their personality, try and pretend to be someone else. And it's ... it's very strange, the way that I think ... you would talk ... you can talk to someone on the Internet, in a way that you would never dream of talking to someone to their face, or on the telephone. If you met them in the street, you would not say the things you say to them on the Internet ... er ... to their face. And it's ... I think it somehow sort of gets rid of the values, possibly, that you hold for people that you meet, because you treat them in a totally different way because you can't ... you can't see them, you can't see how they're reacting. You just go by what they say, and that ... that can be covering up, you know, feelings.

Penny
Well, I think the advent of feminism in the early sixties ... I'm a sort of late fifties baby, so I have really benefitted from that. Er ... I found it really fascinating, I can see obviously it's gone too far in some ways, but for me it's given me the right to have my own life, my own job, a career plus being a mother, ... erm ... the advent of the Pill was obviously a great event as well, ... erm ... which made women feel they have ... they had more control over their bodies, what they wanted to do with their bodies, ... erm ... and that there was a life after children.

Pam
I think a really significant event in this century was the discovery of penicillin. I was told when my first child was born that ... that if I hadn't had antibiotics, I would have died in childbirth, like so many women did before me.

David
Well, the arrival of the motor car erm ... the ... the ... the growth of motoring throughout the twentieth century has ... has changed people's lives. It's changed the whole way that people interact with their relatives, with their friends, business. And, really only in the past ... like in the last twenty years of ... of the century has it been realized that it also brings with it enormous amounts of problems, er .. through

er ... pollution, congestion, erm ... through making people feel too ... too er ... reliant on motor power rather than cycling or walking or erm ... using public transport, even. The balance between using er ... using the car properly, and letting it take over our lives hasn't really been found yet, and that is the big problem for the twenty-first century.

Hilary
It would be very easy to be flippant ... about it, and say it was the Beatles, or something like that, or Elvis. But I suspect it was probably the First World War. I know that was very early ... quite early on in the century, but erm ... I think everybody's life was ... from what I've read, not from personal experience, everybody's life was so changed by that. And the whole structure of society was so changed by that. I think that must be the main change ... the main event of this century. The Second World War was dreadful. It should never have happened and ... but life ... and life certainly was different after it than before, from what I've heard. But not so hugely si ... hugely different as it was before and after the ... Even though the First World War was only four years, it just revolutionized everything. Probably because things were coming to an end before it, anyway, the sort of Edwardian society was rather in decay, anyway, and was ready for a change, but er ... I think life in the 1920s compared with the life in the 1900s was like a different century.

Barry
For me personally ... and don't laugh, because in a way this is silly, but in a way it isn't ... the greatest moment of change in the twentieth century was actually ... Elvis Presley. I remember so well hearing *Heartbreak Hotel*. The first time you heard that – ah! And then suddenly ... I mean, it was more than just a pop record, it was more than just a ... singer ... you know ... a pop singer who's new and different. Suddenly it was ... it was the beginning of youth ... I mean, the whole culture of youth, taking over, which has gone on and on ever since. Suddenly, instead of young people being like and dressing like their mums and dads, and doing what their mums and dads did and gradually drifting into their way of life, nothing very different, suddenly youth had an identity. And it rebelled and challenged and said 'Hey, we're here. You'd better listen to us, because we're going to do what we want for a change.' Youth was nothing before Elvis, was it? I mean, our elders and betters had led us into the Second World War, had ... had created disasters left, right, and centre, had invented the atomic bomb and killed cities full of people, and ... er ... society was ripe for a change. Young people said, 'Right, now it's our turn.'

T12.6

Elvis Presley (1935–1977) was a rock and roll singer whose enormous success changed popular culture throughout the world.

Presley was raised in Memphis, where he sang at church services.

As a teenager, he taught himself to play the guitar.

In July 1954 Presley recorded songs for Sam Phillips, a rhythm and blues producer.

His charismatic style on stage earned him the nickname 'Elvis the Pelvis'.

About this time Presley met Colonel Tom Parker, a promoter who managed the rest of his career.

In 1956 Presley released *Heartbreak Hotel*, the first of 45 records that sold more than a million copies each.

He frequently appeared on television, but because his dancing was considered too sexually suggestive, he was seen only from the waist up.

Presley's personal life suffered desperately, and he fought battles with weight gain and drug dependence.

Before Presley, there were no teenagers, just young people without a voice. He was one of the founders of youth culture.

T12.7

a A Did you see the match last night?
   B No, I missed it, but apparently it was a good game. We won, didn't we?
   A Actually, it was a draw, but it was really exciting.

b A What do you think of Claire's new boyfriend?
   B Personally, I can't stand him. I think she'll be let down by him. However, that's her problem, not mine.
   A Poor old Claire! She always picks the wrong ones, doesn't she? Anyway, I'll see you later. Bye!
   B Bye, Rita.

c A I don't know how you can afford to buy all those fabulous clothes!
   B Hopefully, I'm going to get a bonus this month. I should do. My boss promised it to me. After all, I did earn the company over £100,000 last year. Actually, it was nearer £150,000. I do deserve it, don't you think?
   A Of course you do.

d A She said some horrible things to me. I hate her! She called me names!
   B All the same, I think you should apologize to her.
   A Me? Apologize? Never!
   B Basically, I think you're both being very childish. Why don't you grow up?
   A Oh, Mary! Honestly, I never thought you'd speak to me like that. I hate you, too.

e A So, Billy Peebles. You say that this is the last record you're ever going to make?
   B Definitely.
   A But surely you realize how upset your fans are going to be?
   B Obviously, I don't want to hurt anyone, but basically I'm fed up with pop music. I'd like to do something else. Ideally, I'd like to get into films.
   A Well, we wish you all the best.

Grammar Reference

UNIT 7

Verb patterns

Uses of the *-ing* form

1 The *-ing* form (gerund or present participle) is used after prepositions.
*I'm good **at running**.*
*We're thinking **of living** abroad.*
*I'm interested **in seeing** your book.*
***After having** lunch, we tidied up.*
*I'm looking forward **to meeting** you.*
*We can't get used **to driving** on the left.*

Notice that in the last two examples, *to* is a preposition, so it is followed by *-ing*. It is NOT part of the infinitive.

2 The *-ing* form is used after certain verbs.
*I **enjoy visiting** my relatives.*
*She **denies stealing** the money.*

Here are some other verbs followed by *-ing*.

avoid	admit	finish	can't stand	don't mind
adore	give up	keep on	can't stop	can't help

3 There are some verbs that are followed by an object + *-ing*.
*I **hate people telling** me what to do.*
*You can't **stop me doing** what I want.*
*I can **hear someone playing** the violin.*
*I **spent the weekend gardening**.*
*Don't **waste time doing** nothing.*

4 The *-ing* form is used as the subject or object of a sentence.
***Living** in a big city is exciting.*
***Smoking** is bad for your health.*
*I find **working** in the garden a real bore.*

5 The *-ing* form is used after certain idiomatic expressions.
*It's no use **talking** to her. She never listens.*
*This book is **worth reading**.*
*There's no point in **doing** it your way. It won't work.*
*It's no good **saying** you're sorry. It's not enough.*

Note
suggest can be followed by *-ing* or a *that* clause.
*He suggested **going** to London to look for work.*
*I suggest **(that) we all go** to bed.*

Forms of the infinitive

Present Simple
*I want **to have** a bath.*
*It's time **to go**.*

Present Continuous
*It's nice **to be sitting** here with you.*
*I'd like **to be lying** next to a swimming pool.*
*They seem **to be having** a few problems.*

Perfect
*I'd like **to have seen** his face when you told him.*
*He seems **to have forgotten** about our date.*
*I hope **to have retired** by the time I'm fifty.*

Passive
*I'd like **to be promoted** to sales manager.*
*There's a lot of tidying up **to be done**.*
*I asked **to be informed** as soon as there was any news.*

Note
• These infinitives are used after modal auxiliary verbs without *to*.
*You should **be working**, not watching TV.*
*She must **have gone** home early.*
*This essay must **be done** by tomorrow.*

Uses of the infinitive

1 Infinitives are used after certain verbs.
*I **can't afford to pay** the bill.*
*I **hope to see** you again soon.*
*I **didn't mean to hurt** you.*

Here are some other verbs followed by the infinitive.

agree	attempt	choose	dare	decide	expect	help	want
learn	manage	need	offer	promise	refuse	seem	long

2 There are some verbs that are followed by an object + the infinitive.
*He **advised me to listen** carefully.*
*They **invited her to have** lunch.*

Here are some other verbs like this.

allow	remind	
encourage	teach	someone to do something
order	tell	
persuade	force	

3 There are some verbs that sometimes take an object + the infinitive, and sometimes don't.
*I want **to go** home.*
*I want **you to go** home.*

*I'd like **to help** you.*
*I'd like **you to make** up your own mind.*

Here are some other verbs like this.

ask	beg	
expect	would love	to go
help	would prefer	someone to do something
need	would hate	

Note
help can be used with or without *to*.

She helped me	tidy	up.
	to tidy	

4 The infinitive is used after *make*, *let*, and *allow*.
*She made me **do** the exercise again. (active – without to)*
*I was made **to stand** in the corner. (passive – with to)*
*He let me **go** home. (active – without to)*
*He allowed me **to go** home.*
*I was allowed **to borrow** the car.*

Let in this sense is not possible in the passive. **I was let** ...

5 The infinitive is used after certain adjectives.
*It's **difficult to explain** how to get there.*
*It's **impossible to get** through to her.*
***Pleased to meet** you.*
*I'm **surprised to see** you here.*
*You were **lucky to find** me.*
*Dogs are **easy to train**.*
*It's **good to be** back home.*
*She's **nice to talk** to.*

Note the pattern with *for*.
*It's difficult **for me to explain**.*

6 The infinitive is used after certain nouns.
*It's **time to go**.*
*It's a good **idea to ask** for help.*
*I didn't agree with the **decision to close** down the factory.*
*There's no **need to ask** for permission.*
*My job gives me the **opportunity to travel**.*

7 The infinitive is used to express purpose.
  *I came here **to learn** English.*
  *I need more money **to buy** all the things I want.*

8 The infinitive is used after certain question words. See p 61.
  *I don't know **what to do**.*
  *Can you tell me **how to get** there?*

9 The infinitive can be used with *too* and *enough*.
  *I was **too** tired **to eat**.*
  *There were **too** many people **to get** in the house.*
  *It's cold **enough to snow**.*
  *There isn't **enough** time **to do** all the things I'd like to.*

-*ing* or the infinitive?

continue, start, begin

1 Both -*ing* and the infinitive can be used. The infinitive is more common.

  He began | ***working*** / ***to work*** | *when he was twenty.*

  She continued | ***ironing.*** / ***to iron.***

2 If the verb is in a continuous tense, we prefer the infinitive.
  *It's starting **to rain**.*

3 Certain state verbs are rarely found in continuous tenses. They are also rare in the continuous infinitive.
  *I began **to like** Joan more and more.* *I began liking ...

like, love, hate, prefer

1 Often both -*ing* and the infinitive can be used with little difference of meaning.

  I like | ***to get*** / ***getting*** | *up early.*

  I love | ***to lie*** / ***lying*** | *in the bath.*

2 When *like* means *enjoy generally*, it is more usually followed by -*ing*.
  *I like **cooking**.*

  If the sentence is more specific, the infinitive is more common.
  *I like **to cook** a roast on Sundays.*
  *I like **to read** a book before going to sleep at night.*

3 When *like* means *think it a good idea*, it is followed by the infinitive.
  *I like **to pay** bills on time.*
  *I like **to go** to the dentist regularly.*

4 Used with *would*, these verbs are followed by the infinitive.
  *I'd like **to relax** for a bit.*
  *I'd love **to visit** you.*
  *She'd hate **to be** poor.*
  *We'd prefer **to travel** by train if possible.*

remember, forget, regret

1 After these verbs, the -*ing* form refers to an action that took place *before* the act of remembering, forgetting, or regretting.
  *I remember **having** some lovely holidays when I was a kid.*
  *I'll never forget **meeting** you.*
  *I regret **lying** to her.*

2 The infinitive refers to an action that takes place *after* the act of remembering, forgetting, or regretting.
  *I must remember **to buy** my mother a birthday card.*
  *Don't forget **to lock** all the doors.*
  *I regret **to tell** you that you've failed.*

stop

1 The -*ing* form refers to an action that was in progress *before* the act of stopping.
  *We stopped **playing** tennis because it got too dark.*
  *Stop **looking** at me like that!*

2 The infinitive tells us why the action stopped, and what happened next. This is the infinitive of purpose.
  *We stopped **to have** a break.*
  *Have you ever stopped **to think** how much you spend on cigarettes?*

try

1 The infinitive refers to the goal, or what we want to achieve.
  *I tried **to learn** Chinese, but it was too difficult.*
  *We tried **to put out** the fire, but it was impossible.*

2 The -*ing* form refers to the methods used to achieve the goal.
  *I tried **going** to evening classes.*
  *We tried **pouring** on water, my husband tried **covering** it with a blanket, but it didn't work.*

3 Sometimes there is little or no difference.

  Have you ever tried | ***driving*** / ***to drive*** | *in London?*

UNIT 8

Modal auxiliary verbs

Introduction

1 These are modal auxiliary verbs.

  | can | could | may | might | shall |
  | should | will | would | must | ought to |

  They are used with great frequency and with a wide range of meanings.
  They express ideas such as willingness and ability, permission and refusal, obligation and prohibition, suggestion, necessity, promise and intention. All modal auxiliary verbs can express degrees of certainty, probability, or possibility.

2 They have several characteristics in common.

• There is no -*s* in the third person.
  He can swim.
  She must go.

• There is no *do*/*does* in the question.
  May I ask a question?
  Shall we go?

• There is no *don't*/*doesn't* in the negative.
  You shouldn't tell lies.
  You won't believe this.

• They are followed by an infinitive without *to*. The exception is *ought to*.
  *It might **rain**.*
  *Could you **help**?*
  *We ought **to be** on our way.*

• They don't really have past forms or infinitives or -*ing* forms. Other verbs are used instead.
  *I **had** to work hard when I was young.*
  *I'd love **to be able** to ski.*
  *I hate **having** to get up in the morning.*

• They can be used with perfect infinitives to refer to the past.
  *You should **have told** me that you can't swim.*
  *You might **have drowned**!*
  *She must **have been** crazy to marry him.*

Modal auxiliary verbs of probability, present and future

The main modal auxiliary verbs that express probability are described here in order of certainty. *Will* is the most certain, and *might/could* are the least certain.

will

1 *Will* and *won't* are used to predict a future action. The truth or certainty of what is asserted is more or less taken for granted.
I'll see you later.
His latest book will be out next month.

2 *Will* and *won't* are also used to express what we believe or guess to be true about the present. They indicate an assumption based on our knowledge of people and things, their routines, character, and qualities.
'You've got a letter from Canada.'   'It'll be from my aunt Freda.'
Leave the meat in the oven. It won't be cooked yet.
'I wonder what Sarah's doing.'   'Well, it's Monday morning, so I guess that right now she'll be taking the children to school.'

must and can't

1 *Must* is used to assert what we infer or conclude to be the most logical or rational interpretation of a situation. We do not have all the facts, so it is less certain than *will*.
You say he walked across the Sahara Desert! He must be mad!
You must be joking! I simply don't believe you.

2 The negative of this use is *can't*.
She can't have a ten-year-old daughter! She's only twenty-one herself.
'Whose is this coat?'   'It can't be Mary's. It's too small.'

should

1 *Should* expresses what may reasonably be expected to happen. Expectation means believing that things are or will be as we want them to be. This use of *should* has the idea of *if everything has gone according to plan.*
Our guests should be here soon (if they haven't got lost).
This homework shouldn't take you too long (if you've understood what you have to do).
We should be moving into our new house soon (as long as nothing goes wrong).

2 *Should* in this use has the idea that we want the action to happen. It is not used to express negative or unpleasant ideas.
You should pass the exam. You've worked hard.
*You should fail the exam. You haven't done any work at all.

may and might

1 *May* expresses the possibility that an event will happen or is happening.
We may go to Greece this year. We haven't decided yet.
'Where's Ann?'   'She may be having a bath, I don't know.'

2 *Might* is more tentative and slightly less certain than *may*.
It might rain. Take your umbrella.
'Where's Peter?'   'He might be upstairs. There's a light on.'

3 Learners of English often express these concepts of future possibility with *perhaps* or *maybe ... will* and so avoid using *may* and *might*. However, these are widely used by native speakers, and you should try to use them.

could

1 *Could* has a similar meaning to *might*.
You could be right. I'm not sure.
The film could be worth seeing. It had a good review.

2 *Couldn't* is not used to express a future possibility. The negative of *could* in this use is *might not*.
You might not be right.
The film might not be any good.

3 *Couldn't* has a similar meaning to *can't* above, only slightly weaker.
She couldn't have a ten-year-old daugher! She's only 21 herself.

Modal auxiliary verbs of probability in the past

All the modal auxiliary verbs above can be used with the perfect infinitive. They express the same varying degrees of certainty. Again, *will have done* is the most certain, and *might/could have done* is the least certain.
'I met a tall girl at your party. Very attractive.'   'That'll have been my sister, Patsy.'
It must have been a good party. Everyone stayed till dawn.
The music can't have been any good. Nobody danced.
Where's Pete? He should have been here ages ago!
He may have got lost.
He might have decided not to come.
He could have had an accident.

Other uses of modal auxiliary verbs

Here is some further information about modal auxiliary verbs, but it is by no means complete. See a grammar book if you want more details.

Obligation and advice

1 *Must* expresses strong obligation. Other verb forms are provided by *have to*.
You must try harder!
You mustn't hit your baby brother.
What time do you have to start work?
I had to work hard to pass my exams.
You'll have to do this exercise again.
We might have to make some economies.
She's never had to do a single day's work in her life.
I hate having to get up early.

2 *Must* expresses the opinion of the speaker.
I must get my hair cut. (I am telling myself.)
You must do this again. (Teacher to student)

Must is associated with a more formal, written style.
Candidates must answer three questions. (On an exam paper)
Books must be returned by the end of the week. (Instructions in a library)

Have to expresses a general obligation based on a law or rule, or based on the authority of another person.
Children have to go to school until they're sixteen. (It's the law.)
Mum says you have to tidy your room.

3 *Mustn't* expresses negative obligation. *Don't have to* expresses the absence of obligation.
You mustn't steal. It's very naughty.
You don't have to go to England if you want to learn English.

4 *Have got to* is common in British English. It is more informal than *have to*.
I've got to go now. Cheerio!
Don't have a late night. We've got to get up early tomorrow.

5 *Should* and *ought* express mild obligation or advice. *Should* is much more common.
You should go to bed. You look very tired.
You ought to take things easier.

6 *Should* + the perfect infinitive is used to refer to a past action that didn't happen. The action would have been a good idea. The good advice is too late!

*You **should have listened** to my advice. I was right all the time.*

Permission

1 *May*, *can*, and *could* are used to ask for permission.

May *I ask you a question?*
May *I use your phone?*
Can/could *I go home? I don't feel well.*
Can/Could *I borrow your car tonight?*

2 *May* is used to give permission, but it sounds very formal. *Can* and *can't* are more common.

*You **can** use a dictionary in this exam.*
*You **can't** stay up till midnight. You're only five.*
*You **can't** smoke in here. It's forbidden.*

3 To talk about permission generally, or permission in the past, we use *can*, *could*, or *be allowed to*.

*Children **can/are allowed to** do what they want these days.*

I | **couldn't** / **wasn't allowed to** | *go out on my own until I was sixteen.*

Ability

1 *Can* expresses ability. The past is expressed by *could*.

*I **can** speak three languages.*
*I **could** swim when I was three.*

2 Other forms are provided by *be able to*.

*I've never **been able to** understand her.*
*I love **being able to** drive.*
*You'll **be able to** walk again soon.*

3 To express a fulfilled ability on one particular occasion in the past, *could* is not used. Instead, we use *was able to* or *managed to*.

*She **was able to** survive by clinging onto the wrecked boat.*
*The prisoner **managed to** escape by climbing onto the roof.*

4 *Could* + the perfect infinitive is used to express an unrealized past ability. Someone was able to do something in the past, but didn't try to.

*I **could have gone** to university, but I didn't want to.*
*I **could have told** you that Chris wouldn't come. He hates parties.*

5 *Could* can be used to criticize people for not doing things. We feel that they are not doing their duty.

*You **could** tell me if you're going to be late!*
*You **could have done** something to help me instead of just sitting there!*

Request

Several modal verbs express a request.

Can/could/will/would *you do me a favour?*

Willingness and refusal

1 *Will* expresses willingness. *Won't* expresses a refusal by either people or things. *Shall* is used in questions.

*I'**ll** help you.*
*She says she **won't** get up until she's had breakfast in bed.*
*The car **won't** start.*
Shall *I give you a hand?*

2 The past is expressed by *wouldn't*.

*My mum said she **wouldn't** give me any more money. Isn't she mean?*

Modal auxiliary verbs are also dealt with in Units 10 and 11.

UNIT 9

Questions

what and *which*

1 *What* and *which* are used with nouns to make questions.

What size *shoes do you take?*
Which of these curries *is the hottest?*

2 Sometimes there is no difference between questions with *what* and *which*.

What/which is the biggest city *in your country?*
What/which channel *is the match on?*

We use *which* when the speaker has a limited number of choices in mind.

*There's a blue one and a red one. **Which** do you want?*

We use *what* when the speaker is not thinking of a limited number of choices.

What car *do you drive?*

Asking for descriptions

1 *What is X like?* means *Give me some information about X because I don't know anything about it.*

*What's your capital city **like**?*
*What are your parents **like**?*

2 *How is X?* asks about a person's health and happiness.

How's your mother these days?

3 Sometimes both questions are possible. *What ... like?* asks for objective information. *How ... ?* asks for a more personal reaction.

*'**What** was the party **like**?'   'Noisy. Lots of people. It went on till 3.'*
*'**How** was the party?'   'Brilliant. I danced all night. Met loads of great people.'*

How was your journey?
How's your new job going?
How's your meal?

Indirect questions

There is no inversion and no *do/does/did* in indirect questions.

*I wonder what she's doing. *I wonder ~~what is she doing~~.*
*I don't know where he lives. *I don't know ~~where does he live~~.*
Tell me when the train leaves.
Do you remember how she made the salad?
I didn't understand what she was saying.
I've no idea why he went to India.
I'm not sure where they live.
He doesn't know whether he's coming or going.

Negatives

Forming negatives

1 We make negatives by adding *not* after the auxiliary verb. If there is no auxiliary verb, we add *do/does/did*.

*I **haven't** seen her for ages.*
*It **wasn't** raining.*
*You **shouldn't** have gone to so much trouble.*
*We **don't** like big dogs.*
*They **didn't** want to go out.*

2 The verb *have* has two forms in the present.

*I **don't** have* | *any money.*
*I **haven't** got* |

*But ... I **didn't** have any money.*

3 Infinitives and *-ing* forms can be negative.

*We decided **not to do** anything.*

*I like **not working**. It suits me.*

4   *Not* can go with other parts of a sentence.
*Ask him, **not me**.*
*Buy me anything, but **not perfume**.*

5   When we introduce negative ideas with verbs such as *think*, *believe*, *suppose*, and *imagine*, we make the first verb negative, not the second.
*I **don't think** you're right. *~~I think you aren't~~ ...*
*I **don't suppose** you want a game a tennis?*

6   In short answers, the following forms are possible.
'Are you coming?'   'I think so.'
                    'I believe so.'
                    'I hope so.'
                    'I don't think so.'
                    'I hope not.'

I think not is possible. *~~I don't hope so~~ is not possible.*

Negative questions

1   In the main use of negative questions, the speaker would normally expect a positive situation, but now expects a negative situation. The speaker therefore is surprised.
*Don't you **like** ice-cream? Everyone likes ice-cream!*
*Haven't you **done** your homework yet? What have you been doing?*

2   Negative questions can also be used to mean *confirm what I think is true*. In this use it refers to a positive situation.
*Haven't I **met** you somewhere before? (I'm sure I have.)*
*Didn't we **speak** about this yesterday? (I'm sure we did.)*

The difference between the two uses can be seen clearly if we change them into question tags.
*You **haven't done** your homework yet, **have you**? (negative sentence, positive tag)*
*We've **met** before, **haven't we**? (positive sentence, negative tag)*

UNIT 10

Expressing habit

Present Simple

1   Adverbs of frequency come before the main verb, but after the verb *to be*.
*We **hardly ever** go out.*
*She **frequently** forgets what she's doing.*
*We don't **usually** eat fish.*
*I **rarely** see Peter these days.*
*We are **seldom** at home in the evening.*
*Is he **normally** so bad-tempered?*

2   *Sometimes*, *usually*, and *occasionally* can come at the beginning or the end of a sentence.
Sometimes we play cards.
*We go to the cinema **occasionally**.*

The other adverbs of frequency don't usually move in this way.
~~Always I have~~ tea in the morning.

Present Continuous

1   The Present Continuous can be used to express a habit which happens often and perhaps unexpectedly. It happens more than is usual.
*I like Peter. He's always **smiling**.*
*She's always **giving** people presents.*

2   However, there is often an element of criticism with this structure. Compare these sentences said by a teacher.
*Pedro always **asks** questions about the lesson. (This is a fact.)*

*Pedro **is always asking** questions about the lesson. (This annoys the teacher.)*

3   There is usually an adverb of frequency with this use.
*I'm always **losing** my keys.*
*She's **forever leaving** the bath taps running.*

will and would

1   *Will* and *would* express typical behaviour. They describe both pleasant and unpleasant habits.
He'll sit in his chair all day long.
She'd spend all day long gossiping with the neighbours.

2   *Will* and *would*, when decontracted and stressed, express an annoying habit.
*He **WILL** come into the house with his muddy boots on.*
*She **WOULD** make us wash in ice-cold water.*

used to + infinitive

1   This structure expresses a past action and state. It has no present equivalent.
*When I was a child, we **used to go** on holiday to the seaside.*

2   Notice the negative and the question.
*Where **did** you **use** to go?*
*We **didn't use** to do anything interesting.*

3   We cannot use *used to* with a time reference + a number.
~~We used to have a holiday there for 10 years/three times~~.
But ...
*We **used to** go there every year.*

be/get used to + noun/-ing form

1   This is totally different from *used to* + infinitive. It expresses an action that was difficult, strange, or unusual before, but is no longer so. Here, *used* is an adjective, and it means *familiar with*.
*I found it difficult to get around London when I first came, but **I'm used to it** now.*
*I'm **used to getting** around London by tube.*

2   Notice the use of *get* to express the process of change.
*I'm **getting used to** the climate.*
*I'm **getting used to** eating with chopsticks.*

UNIT 11

Hypothesizing

First and second conditionals

1   First conditional sentences are based on fact in real time. They express a possible condition and its probable result in the present or future.
*If you **pass** your exams, **I'll buy** you a car.*

2   Second conditional sentences are not based on fact. They express a situation which is contrary to reality in the present and future. This unreality is shown by a tense shift from present to past. They express a hypothetical condition and its probable result.
*If I **were** taller, **I'd join** the police force.*
*What **would** you **do** if you **won** the lottery?*

Notes
•   The difference between first and second conditional sentences is not about time. Both can refer to the present and future. By using past tense forms in the second conditional, the speaker suggests the situation is less probable, or impossible, or imaginary.

Compare the pairs of sentences.
*If it **rains** this weekend, we'll ... (Said in England where it often rains.)*
*If it **rained** in the Sahara, it **would** ... (This would be most unusual.)*

*If there **is** a nuclear war, we'll ...* (I'm a pessimist.)
*If there **was** a nuclear war, we'd ...* (I'm an optimist.)

*If you **come** to my country, you'll **have** a good time.* (Possible)
*If you **came** from my country, you'd **understand** us better.* (Impossible)

*If I **am elected** as a member of Parliament, I'll ...* (Said by a candidate)
*If I **ruled** the world, I'd ...* (Imaginary)

- We can use *were* instead of *was*, especially in a formal style.
  *If I **were** you, I'd get some rest.*
  *I'd willingly help if it **were** possible.*

Third conditional

Third conditional sentences are not based on fact. They express a situation which is contrary to reality in the past. This unreality is shown by a tense shift from past to Past Perfect.

*If you'd **come** to the party, you'd **have had** a great time.*
*I **wouldn't have met** my wife if I **hadn't gone** to France.*

Note

It is possible for each of the clauses in a conditional sentence to have a different time reference, and the result is a mixed conditional.

*If we **had brought** a map* (we didn't), *we **would know** where we are* (we don't).
*I **wouldn't have married** her* (I did) *if I **didn't love** her* (I do).

Other structures that express hypothesis

The tense usage with *wish*, *if only*, and *I'd rather* is similar to the second and third conditionals. Unreality is expressed by a tense shift.

*I wish I **were** taller.* (But I'm not.)
*If only you **hadn't said** that!* (But you did.)
*I'd rather you **didn't smoke**.* (But you do.)

Notes

- *wish ... would* can express regret, dissatisfaction, impatience, or irritation because someone WILL keep doing something.
  I wish you'd stop smoking.
  I wish you'd do more to help in the house.
  *I wish it **would** stop raining.*

- If we are not talking about willingness, *wish ... would* is not used.
  I wish my birthday wasn't in December. (*I ~~wish it would be~~ ...)
  I wish I could stop smoking. (*I ~~wish I would~~* is strange because you should have control over what you are willing to do.)
  I wish he would stop smoking. (This is fine because it means *I wish he were willing to ...*)

should have done

1 *Should* + the perfect infinitive is used to refer to a past action that didn't happen. The action would have been a good idea. It is advice that is too late!
  *You **should have come** to the party!* (But you didn't.)
  *You **shouldn't have called** him a fool.* (But you did.)

2 It is also used to refer to an action that might or might not have happened in the past. This use is dealt with in Unit 8.
  *It's 10.00. They **should have arrived** by now.*

UNIT 12

Noun phrases

Adding information to nouns

1 Adjectives come before a noun.
  red *roses*   *a* **thatched** *roof*

  Two- and three-part adjectives are hyphenated before a noun.
  a **grey-haired** *businessman*
  an **open-air** *pool*
  a **three-year-old** *girl*

2 Nouns can be joined to make compound nouns.
  swimming pool   *parking ticket*
  football boots   *traffic warden*

3 Relative clauses and participle clauses come after a noun. These are dealt with in Unit 6.
  a driving licence **which expires soon**
  a boy **licking an ice-cream**
  football boots **stuffed in a bag**

4 Phrases with a preposition come after a noun.
  a cottage **with** *roses growing* **round** *the door*
  the road **down** *to the beach*
  a man **with** *a briefcase* **in** *his hand*

Articles

The use of articles is complex as there are a lot of 'small' rules and exceptions. Here are the basic rules.

a/an

1 We use *a/an* to refer to a singular countable noun which is indefinite. Either we don't know which one, or it doesn't matter which one.
  *They live in **a** lovely house.*
  *I'm reading **a** good book.*
  *She's expecting **a** baby.*

2 We use *a/an* with professions.
  *She's **a** lawyer.*

the

1 We use *the* before a singular or plural noun, when both the speaker and the listener know which noun is being referred to.
  *They live in **the** green house opposite the library.*
  ***The** book was recommended by a friend.*
  *Mind **the** baby! She's near the fire.*
  *I'm going to **the** shops. Do you want anything?*
  *I'll see you in **the** pub later.*
  *'Where's Dad?' 'In **the** garden.'*

2 We use *the* when there is only one.
  the *world*   **the** *River Thames*   **the** *Atlantic*

3 We use *the* for certain places which are institutions. Which particular place isn't important.
  *We went to **the** cinema/theatre last night.*
  *We're going to **the** seaside.*

zero article

1 We use no article with plural and uncountable nouns when talking about things in general.
  ***Computers** have changed our lives.*
  ***Love** is eternal.*
  ***Dogs** need a lot of exercise.*
  *I hate **hamburgers**.*

2 We use no article with meals.
   *Have you had **lunch** yet?*
   *Come round for **dinner** tonight.*
   But ... *We had **a** lovely lunch in an Italian restaurant.*

Determiners

Determiners that express quantity are dealt with in Unit 4.

each and *every*

1 *Each* and *every* are used with singular nouns. *Each* can be used to talk about two or more people or things. *Every* is used to talk about three or more.
   ***Every/each** time I come to your house it looks different.*
   ***Each/every** bedroom in our hotel is decorated differently.*

2 In many cases, *each* and *every* can both be used with little difference in meaning.
   We prefer *each* if we are thinking of people or things separately, one at a time. We use *every* if we are thinking of the things or people all together as a group.
   ***Each** student gave the teacher a present.*
   ***Every** policeman in the country is looking for the killer.*

Adding emphasis

Word order and the passive

1 An unmarked word order is where all the parts of a sentence are in a 'non-special' order.
   The company presented Kevin with a gold watch on his retirement in 1995.

2 This order can be altered to bring different elements to a stronger position in the sentence.
   ***On his retirement in 1995**, the company presented Kevin with a gold watch.*
   ***In 1995**, the company presented Kevin with a gold watch on his retirement.*

3 Using the passive shifts the focus of attention onto the object of the active sentence.
   *On his retirement in 1995, **Kevin was presented** with a gold watch.*
   Often, *by* + the agent is not used in passive sentences. On the occasions when it is, it is in a strong position in the sentence.
   *On his retirement, Kevin was presented with a gold watch **by the chairman of the board**.*
   *A country's food is largely influenced **by the climate**.*
   *Entertainment on board ship will be provided **by the well-known singer and comedian, Gary Weeks**.*

Emphatic structures

Sentences can be reordered and introduced by certain structures to make the important information stand out.
***What I like about London is the fact that** it never sleeps.*
***What annoys me about Gerald is** his arrogance.*
***The thing that annoys me about Gerald is** his arrogance.*
***It's people like you who** spoil things for everyone else.*

Emphasis and speaking

1 We can use our voice to stress the important part of a sentence.
   'Where did you get that car from?'   *'**Peter** gave it to me.'*
   'Did he sell it to you?'   *'No, he **gave** it to me.'*
   'I want it.'   *'Tough. He gave it to **me**.'*

2 If we want to express a contrast on the idea expressed by the verb, we stress the auxiliary. If there is no auxiliary, we add *do/does/did*.
   *She told me to clean my room, but **I have** cleaned it.*
   'Don't get angry.'   *'**I am** angry.'*
   'Why weren't you at the party?'   *'**I was** at the party.'*
   'What a shame you don't like ice-cream.'   *'**I do** like ice-cream.'*
   'Why didn't he give you a present?'   *'He **did** give me a present. Look.'*

Acknowledgements

The authors would like to express their sincere thanks and appreciation to the following people who have all helped in the production of this book:

The students in our class at International House, London, who tried the book out with us and gave us valuable feedback. We had a lot of fun together: Annick Montoulieu (France); Naohiro Nobuta (Japan); Lori Eidelsztein (Argentina); Kaori Sato (Japan); Shirlei Bortoleto (Brazil); Gonul Kartal (Turkey); Son Ke-Young (Korea); Andrei Nissen (Brazil); Selma Rio Goncalves (Brazil); Fernando Borges D. Furtado (Brazil); Luiz Henrique Coelho Baeta (Brazil); Zofia Przednowek (Poland).

Justin Baines for his clever and witty maze; Guy Heath for his suggestions for the vocabulary in Unit 7; Richard Carrington, Paul Gillingham, David Griffiths, and Sarah Rosewarne for their research and recordings of people in all walks of life; Natalie Hodgson, Jo Devoy, Tom and Sue Higgins, Megan and Kate Soars for agreeing to be interviewed; Fiona Goble for her short story Things we never said.

Everyone at OUP for their unfailing encouragement, support, and enthusiasm: Sylvia Wheeldon (Managing Editor), Elana Katz (Senior Editor), Sally Lack (Producton Editor), Jane Havis (Designer), Sara Gray (Art Editor), Peter Marsh (Audio Producer), Pearl Bevan (Senior Design Project Manager). They were a great team!

The publisher and authors are very grateful to the following teachers and institutions for reading and/or piloting the manuscript, and for providing invaluable comment and feedback on the course:

Beyhan Aytekin; Danuta Domaradzka; David Doyle; Robert Fenlon; David Horner; Bernie Hayden; Frank Lajkó; Mike Mansell; Roger Marshall; David Massey; Szilvia Mándli Portöro; Iain K. Robinson; Michael John Sayer; Martin Toal.

Language Centre of Ireland, Dublin; Eckersley School of English, Oxford; European Language Schools, Vigo; Révai Miklós Gimnázium, Gyòr; International House, Budapest; József Attila Gimnázium; Budapest; Escola d'Idiomes Moderns, Universitat de Barcelona; TÖMER, Ankara; Facultad de Idiomas, Universidad Veracruzana.

The authors and publisher would like to thank the following for permission to reproduce extracts and adaptations of copyright material:

Sean Blair for extracts from his article 'Icy Hell' from Focus, February 1997.

Jess McAree for extracts from the article 'Does the black box still do its job?' from Focus, July 1996.

Ewan MacNaughton Associates on behalf of the Telegraph Group Limited for extracts from Michael Schmidt: 'The Woman who made £17m from only £5' Daily Telegraph, 13 June 1996; Charles Laurence; 'I'll marry you, but only if we can …' Daily Telegraph, 14 February 1996.

Robert Matthews for adapted extracts from his articles 'The hundred weirdest mysteries known to science' from Focus, August 1996 and September 1996.

News International Syndication on behalf of Times Newspapers Limited for extracts from Peter Millar: 'I am become Death, the destroyer of worlds' from The Sunday Times Magazine, 16 July 1995, © Times Newspapers Limited, 1995.

The Observer for extracts from 'King of the Eccentrics' from The Observer Magazine, 17 January 1993, © The Observer, 1993.

Pan Books for use of 'The Third Twin' by Ken Follett.

Reed Books for extracts from Nigel Blundell: 'The World's Greatest Mistakes' (Octopus, a division of Reed Consumer Books Ltd).

Solo Syndication for extracts from Stewart Payne: 'Living History' Evening Standard 18 July 1994; Mary Greene: 'Money - has it become the eighth deadly sin?' Daily Mail Weekend, 12 June 1995; Melissa Jones: 'The Great Escape' Daily Mail Weekend, 11 May 1996; Chris Parker: 'There's no place like our home' Daily Mail Weekend, I June 1996; Giles Minton: 'Does tourism destroy everything it touches?' Mail on Sunday, 19 May 1996; Tanya Reed: 'You can't come into Harrods dressed like that' Mail on Sunday, 18 August 1994.

Nicola Tyrer for extracts from her article 'They have nine TV sets …' from the Daily Telegraph, 26 October 1995.

The Week for extracts from 'The man who could own 100,000 Ferraris' from The Week, 22 February 1997.

Fast Car words and music by Tracy Chapman © 1988 EMI April Music Inc/Purple Rabbit Music, USA, reproduced by permission of EMI Songs Ltd, London WC2H 0EA.

Hello Muddah, Hello Fadduh words and music by Allan Sherman and Lou Busch © 1997 Warner Bros Music Corporation, 50% Warner Chappell Music Ltd, 50% unknown publisher.

Waiting at the Church words by Fred W Leigh, music by Henry E Pether © 1906 Francis Day & Hunter Ltd, London WC2H 0EA, reproduced by IMP Ltd.

Every endeavour has been made to identify the sources of all material used. The publisher apologizes for any omissions.

Illustrations by:

Veronica Bailey pp 64, 110; Jon Berkeley p 61; Neil Gower pp 89, 106; Emily Hare pp 99, 108; Lorraine Harrison pp 42, 43; Jane Havis pp 12, 15, 34, 66, 79, 107; John Holder pp 31,32, 33; Ian Kellas pp 8, 13, 22, 26, 27, 37, 38, 47, 49, 54, 58, 60, 68, 71, 74, 76, 77, 79, 80, 87, 88, 89, 94, 95, 97, 98, 100, 108 (Tom), 114, 115, 118, 127; Anne Magill, The Inkshed p 96; Ian Mitchell pp 72, 73; Sarah Perkins, The Inkshed p 51

Handwriting by Kathy Baxendale pp 6, 7, 14, 15, 68, 86, 115

Studio photography by:

Mark Mason pp 6, 7, 14, 15, 18, 24, 25, 29, 30 (Thomas Hardy novels) 35, 39 (coins), 40, 52, 53, 55, 56, 57, 68, 70, 77, 86, 90, 101 (money), 115

Location Photography by:

Maggie Milner p 47
Haddon Davies pp 69, 78 (woman in bed), p 111

The publisher would like to thank the following for their permission to reproduce photographs and copyright material:

Ace Photo Agency p 10 (H Hoffman/Family); Associated Press p 125 (Napalm Attack, Vietnam); Axiom p 16 (Traveller); BBC Picture Archives p 82 (Clapper board - Pride and Prejudice) (filming lights - Pride and Prejudice) (Mr Darcy - Pride and Prejudice) (Clapper board 744 - Pride and Prejudice) (Making of Pride and Prejudice); Bridgeman Art Library p 119 Sistine Chapel Ceiling (1508–12): Creation of Adam, 1511 (detail of Adam by Michelangelo Buonarroti (1475–1564)) Vatican Museums and Galleries, Vatican City, Italy; Bubbles Photolibrary p 95 (Elizabeth, head and shoulders); Collection japonaise/Magnum Photos p 122 (Kikuchi/devastation by first explosion of the atom bomb); The J Allen Cash Photolibrary p 104 (The Taxman - male office worker on phone); Comstock p 75, p 90 (Man eating Hot dog); Corbis UK Ltd p 84 (Marlee Martin holds Oscar), p 112 (Romantic Couple); Daily Mail p 103 (P Davies/divorced mother with 4 kids); Dewynters p 85 (Phantom, Jesus, Cats); Greg Evans p 11 (M Wells/Family), 15 (girl), 66,67 (G Balfour/Restaurants, G Balfour/Shaftesbury Ave, G Balfour/Berwick St Market); Mary Evans Picture Library p 16 (D Livingstone), p 30 (T Hardy); Jimmy Gaston pp 72, 73, B Sell, Reuters, p 81 (Jane Austen); Genesis Photolibrary p 125 (First man on the moon); Getty Images p 10 (Rockies), p 11 (B Marsden/Greek Scene), p 19 (L Gordon/Cave Painting, C Ehlers/Grand Canyon, O Soot/Machu Picchu), p 41 (W Jacobs/Arab Market), p 70 (Evacuee), p 72 (K Hutton/domestic scene), p 95 (B Torrez/Nicole, head and shoulders), p 109 (K Fisher/Holly Harper - Magazine Editor), p 105 (P Tweedie/homeless people huddled together on pavement), p 100 (Two girls on beach, black and white image), p 116 (old sepia print of great aunt with baby); The Ronald Grant Archive p 36; Robert Harding Picture Library p 39 (female portrait); Tom & Sue Higgins p 45; Natalie Hodgson p 24; The Image Bank p 14 (T Schmitt/Sao Paulo), p 16 (M Schneps/Map), p 17 (J F Podevin), p 19 (C Brown/Petra), pp 20, 45 (abstract), p 49 (K Philpot), p 56 (Durham), p 67; Jonathan Knowles p 80 (Man on phone); Pictor Uniphoto p 14 (male portrait), p 28 (Harrods), p 41 (Stock Market), p 47 (Rotterdam), pp 50, 62 (Antarctica), p 95 (George, head and shoulders); Popperfoto/Reuter I Waldie, Reuters, p 120 (Princess Diana arrives at the Royal Albert Hall), p 81 (Emma Thompson with Oscar), p 125 (JFK's assassination), p 125 (Blériot over England), p 126 (The young Elvis); Pictures Library p 15 (Basle), p 30 (Hardy's cottage), p 45 (fish & chips), p 66 (New Year); Popperfoto p 58 (A Bolante/Reuters); Quadrant p 63 (black box); Rex Features p 59, D Cooper, p 85 (Jesus Christ Superstar), J Witt, p 125 (release of Nelson Mandela), R Wallis, p 125 (collapse of the Berlin Wall), p 85 (Tim Rice), p 102 (Chrissie Lytton-Cobbold), p 125 (Diana, Princess of Wales - funeral procession); Science Photo Library p 121 (The first atomic bomb), Los Alamos National Laboratory, p 121 (detonation of the world's first atomic bomb); Tom Scott p 9; Robert Stigwood Organisation Ltd p 85 (Evita); Solo Syndication p 28 (Gilly Woodward), p 99 (K Towner/Rosemary Sage), p 104 (The Miser); Still Pictures p 21; Sygma p 62 (D Hudson/Mangle-Wurzle); Telegraph Colour Library, I McKinnell, p 92 (Starfield (illustration), S J Benbow, p 105 (Male homeless person), p 91 (Planets/Stars); Victoria and Albert Museum p 70 (paper).

The publishers would like to thank the following for their help and assistance:

Jonathan Altaras Associates; Browns Restaurant, Oxford; Oxford Antique Trading Co.; Bank of England.

Oxford University Press, Great Clarendon Street, Oxford OX2 6DP

Oxford   New York

Athens   Auckland   Bangkok   Bogotá
Buenos Aires   Calcutta   Cape Town   Chennai
Dar es Salaam   Delhi   Florence   Hong Kong
Istanbul   Karachi   Kuala Lumpur   Madrid
Melbourne   Mexico City   Mumbai   Nairobi
Paris   São Paulo   Shanghai   Singapore   Taipei
Tokyo   Toronto   Warsaw

and associated companies in
Berlin   Ibadan

OXFORD and OXFORD ENGLISH
are trade marks of Oxford University Press
ISBN 0 19 435 800 3 Complete Edition
ISBN 0 19 435 805 4 Student's Book A
ISBN 0 19 435 806 2 Student's Book B
© Oxford University Press 1998
Second impression 2000

Typeset by Oxford University Press

Printed in China.